Up the Trail from Texas

UP THE TRAIL

FROM TEXAS

———————— ★ ————————

by J. FRANK DOBIE

Illustrated by JOHN C. WONSETLER

Landmark BOOKS

RANDOM HOUSE · NEW YORK

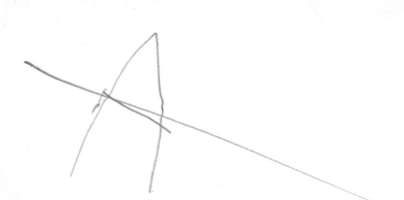

To Frank Dobie Faulk, hoping he will be a bigger man than the one for whom he is named, with affection that includes his father and mother.

Contents

Up the Trail from Texas

"The trail is poetry; a wagon road is prose; the railroad, arithmetic."—John R. Craig, Ranching with Lords and Commons.

1

Up the Trail with Mossy Horns

Gay cowboys dressed in silk and silver rode over the fenceless grass and sang their way up the long cattle trails; cattle kings ruled over ranges as big as European principalities and had feuds with sheep kings. Princesses waiting to be queens were coming out of the castles; villains were behind the bushes. That is the picture-show version.

In reality, when the wholesale driving of Texas cattle north began, cattle kings did not exist. Ranch

homes, mostly small frame houses, were on unfenced lands to which anybody's cattle came and
from which the owner's strayed. The manner of
controlling them was not in the least kingly. The
cowboys were neighborhood friends, and they
had no more finery about them than a wagonload
of cottonpickers.

Their "foppery," like that of Cyrano de Ber-
gerac, was "of the inner man." They had a spirit
incorporating pride and loyalty that could never
come from money or money-bought objects. Neither they nor the owners of the cattle had money.
Something of their spirit came from fidelity to
"the Lost Cause," for most of them were fresh
from the Confederate Army; something of the
spirit came also from the self reliance of the frontier, and something of it had been added by life
on horseback.

Let us look at a crew of trail drivers following
a herd the year after the Civil War ended. The
view is through the eyes of one of the crew named
John Shepherd. At the breakup of the war he was
a private soldier in a company consisting of only
eight men and a third lieutenant under Captain
John H. Robinson. Their army property consisted of six mules—two big ones and four little
ones. Captain Robinson decided to distribute the

mules to the disbanding soldiers—the only bonus their wrecked government could afford. Four soldiers got a little mule apiece; then the captain paired off the other four and assigned a big mule to each pair. John Shepherd and his brother Dan got a big mule.

They came home to their father's little ranch on the Texas frontier, and there John traded off his one-half interest in the big mule to his brother for Dan's stock of cattle—between twenty-five and thirty head scattered over the open range. John was still only twenty years old when about March 1, 1866, he set out with nine other hands to drive 600 big longhorned steers to St. Louis.

There was not a pair of boots or a pair of leggings (chaps) in the outfit. Some of the men wore big-roweled Mexican spurs and some wore little spurs; some had homemade rawhide reatas, some grass ropes. Their clothes had been woven and sewed by the women of their homes. Slickers had not yet come into use. John Shepherd alone among the hands had a Mexican blanket—a poncho with a hole slit in the middle for the head to go through. It would turn water if there was not too much.

Nobody had more than the lightest of bedding. Most of the cowboys had learned to rustle grass and weeds for a bed. If the weather was stormy or rai.iy, they did not need beds anyhow, as at such times they would be on herd to prevent the cattle from drifting or running. They had only two horses apiece for the trip. Shepherd had a mule and a horse. The extra horses were drifted along with the cattle.

The grub consisted of corn meal, salt bacon, beans, coffee, and sorghum molasses. No sugar, nothing in cans. After the herd reached Missouri, the hands gathered wild blackberries and the boss bought sugar and sometimes milk from farmers. At the same time the lanky longhorns filled out on corn bought at ten cents a bushel. Some things happened between the Lockhart prairies in Texas and the cowpens in St. Louis, but the point here is the homely simplicity of life among early trail drivers.

They are all gone now, but when I was young I knew many of them and took down the stories that some told. None was more representative than James Philip Towns. He was born on the Guadalupe River in southern Texas in 1852 in a log cabin built on land that had been granted to his grandfather for services rendered to the Republic of Texas. He still owned a part of the grant when he died. Genial and gigantic, soft-spoken and iron-limbed, as erect as an Indian warrior, white-headed and white-hatted, he was at once mellow with memories and perfectly at ease in this modern world of machinery. Unlike many of the old range riders, he adapted himself to the changes of time.

"Right after the Civil War closed," he said, "I had the greatest disappointment of my life. My mother said to me, 'Jim, hitch the oxen to the cart and take a load of roasting ears to Gonzales and trade them for something to eat. Anyway, bring back a sack of salt.'

"Well, after a drive of a day and a half, moving along as slow as molasses in January, I got to Gonzales. I spent another day driving around and around Gonzales trying to sell or trade off those roasting ears. Finally I swapped a few dozen ears to a traveling photographer for a tintype picture of myself. It was a sad-looking picture, for I had cried a lot over my dismal failure. It seemed there was not a dollar's worth of money or a spoonful of salt in Gonzales. I was forced to go back home without anything but the roasting ears and the tintype. On the whole trip I did not eat anything but corn roasted in ashes."

Beginning in 1869, Towns made seven or eight trips up the trail. The one he remembered most vividly was in 1873. Dunn Houston and George W. Littlefield sent him to receive 3,150 steers they had bought from the noted Shanghai Pierce and two partners. The steers were from three to fifteen years old, of all colors between white and black, some even blue, and they were as wild as antelopes. All had long horns and many horns were ringed and scaly with age. "Mossy horns," the old ones were called, but they were young in fight and vinegar.

Towns had ten cowboys to handle the herd. After he had counted the steers, Bob Stafford told him he would never on earth get them out of the country. "Why," he said, "we've sold and delivered these old scalawags so many times that we're getting ashamed to look at them. They get away from everybody who tries to drive them off. You never saw such a bunch for stampeding, and when they hit one of these brakes, they are gone."

"Well," Towns answered, "I've got some mighty good men to handle them. They are contracted to the Indian Agency at Fort Sill in the Indian Territory, and I don't see anything else to do but deliver them."

"All right, young man," Stafford said, "go ahead. But you'd better have your life insured and get all you can on your men. These cattle will run over you before you have gone a hundred miles."

"As insurance companies would not risk the lives of cowboys in those days and as no cowboy wanted insurance anyhow," Towns told the story, "I did not follow Stafford's advice. We drove the cattle as hard as we could the first day, and that night we milled them around and around so as to tire them out.

"It was on a Sunday morning when we neared the Webberville crossing on the Colorado River. Webberville was just a wide place in the road. A seedy farmer riding an old plow mare wearing a blind bridle offered to pilot us through the bottom. We had to go down a lane made by picket fences that enclosed some fields, and as we got opposite one of the houses a dog rushed out barking. Bedlam broke loose right there.

"Those steers all jumped at once, and as the lane was too narrow for the whole herd to run forward in, a lot of them broke through the fences into the fields. The old farmer was in front. He had a pair of rawhide hobbles that he was using for a quirt, and the way he quirted was a caution. He finally managed to cut off and get out of the way. When the run was over, I offered to pay him for his piloting if he would go on across the river. He said no, he ought to have been at church instead of trying to make a dollar on Sunday. He was convinced that our trouble was a kind of judgment on him and us too for breaking the Sabbath, and he sure wasn't going to invite further 'visitation.'

"About the time we got the herd milling, here came a posse of citizens with a deputy. The deputy said that my steers had ruined the corn fields and that he was going to put me in jail and take charge of them. I told him maybe he could jail me but before he took charge of the herd he'd have to put up a big bond. He had not thought about that. I finally paid the citizens a twenty-dollar gold piece for damages.

"But I was not through with that Webberville bunch. When we counted the cattle, we found we were sixty or seventy short. I felt confident that some of the citizens had cut them off in the brush. With two hands I went back and struck the trail. We found the steers in a pen. Maybe it was a good thing we saw nobody about the pen. We took the steers.

"The herd got the habit of running every night about eleven o'clock. A herd will acquire a habit that way, just like a person with insomnia waking up at a certain hour. As it was a dry year and waterings were scarce, the cattle were often fever-

Bedlam broke loose as the steers all jumped at once

ish. We could draw water at dug wells for the horses where cattle could not be watered.

"As we were approaching Red River, Dunn Houston caught up with us. He had heard about the stampede at Webberville and was mighty uneasy. I had no more than quieted his fears when the thirsty steers sniffed water. They stampeded and scattered for miles up and down the river. Finally we got them together and across into the Indian Nation. Here we struck another dry stretch. The wind was from the south, and after we had gone about twenty miles the cattle either scented the water behind them or else remembered it. Anyway, they turned back. We simply could not hold them.

"Some of them ran that whole twenty miles. They jumped over a bluff that the horses could not go down, recrossed the river, and banked up under the opposite bluff. The men had to pull off their clothes, swim over, and scare the crazy animals back to the north side. The water was strongly impregnated with gyp, or alkali. Dunn Houston swallowed so much that he became violently ill and by night was in such agony with cramps that I thought he would die. I made a poultice out of the ashes of buffalo chips and applied it to his stomach, but it seemed to do no good.

"Then I remembered an adobe hut several miles off that I had ridden past during the day. A squaw man lived there. I rode to this hut and asked for medicine. The man said he had some paregoric and brought out a bottle about half full. I ran my horse all the way back to camp. Thinking that if a little of the medicine would do good, all of it would do better, I poured the whole bottle down Dunn's throat. Very soon he was asleep, and the next day he sent a rider to Fort Sill with notice that we would deliver the cattle on time.

"Colonel Hunter of the Indian Agency was there to receive them. There were a number of three-year-old steers in the herd, and as these brought four dollars a head less than the aged steers, the stuff had to be classified. Colonel Hunter savied cows pretty well, and he had a pocket full of cigars that he was liberal with, but he wore a linen duster and did not look like a cowman. Also he was a Northerner.

"After we had been cutting and classifying steers nearly all day, we still had forty or fifty head to trim.* It was getting close to sundown

* To separate or part, "cut" being the range term.

and the little bunch was hard to hold. Everybody and everybody's horse was dead tired. I was trying to cut a three-year-old steer into a bunch of aged steers and get him by Colonel Hunter. I scared the whole bunch over against a feller named Wekker. His horse was absolutely played out, and when Wekker spurred him, he kicked up and two or three animals got by him.

"At this, Hunter yelled out, 'There now. I've been expecting you to play hob all evening.'

"Wekker was ringy anyhow. 'Give me any more of your talk,' he said, 'and I'll make a sieve out of your blue belly.'

"Colonel Hunter quieted down then. He wasn't mad. He knew well enough he couldn't talk to a Texas cowboy like a slave, and he was a good sport.

"After the last steer was counted over, I rode up to him and said: 'Colonel, I want to tell you something about this herd. They are a bad lot. We bought them a-running, we have driven them clear across Texas a-running, and you can see for yourself that we delivered them a-running. Unless you post your men and ring-herd them* tonight, they will be a-running at eleven o'clock.'

"'Young man,' Colonel Hunter replied, 'I have

* Keep them going in a circle.

bought and handled more Texas cattle than you ever saw. My men will take care of them all right. Here are a few more cigars for your good intentions.'

"That night when Dunn Houston went to bed, he said to me: 'Jim, wake me up at eleven o'clock. I want to hear those steers run at some other fellow's expense.' Sure enough, exactly at eleven P.M. I shook Dunn and told him hell was popping. The last we heard of those old mossy-horns, they were still a-running."

This was just one of many, many drives with Texas longhorns. Their history dates back centuries before the trails they beat out came to be marked on maps of western America.

2

The First Cattle and Horses

There were no cattle or horses in the hemisphere that Columbus discovered. On his second voyage, in 1493, he landed Spanish cattle and horses, with colonists, on the island of Santo Domingo. Other seed stock were introduced over the West Indies, and within a short time their multiplication made ranches a fact. European horses and cattle found the Western Hemisphere as congenial as European human beings found it. They bred as rapidly as money out at compound interest.

In 1519, having sailed from Cuba, Cortés landed the first horses on the North American continent and with them began the conquest of Mexico. Two years later one of his followers landed the first cattle. When Coronado began his expedition into what is now New Mexico in 1540, only twenty-one years after the Spaniards landed on the Mexican coast, he gathered up five hundred head of cattle to supply meat for his followers, and they rode on a thousand horses—most

Spaniards brought horses and cattle to North America

of which had been raised on Mexican ranches. Wherever the Spaniards established missions or settlements, they introduced horses and cattle, along with sheep, goats, hogs, and chickens.

By the time of the American Revolution, Spain had settlements, with horses and cattle, scattered across the continent from San Augustine on the coast of Florida to Los Angeles on the Pacific. Louisiana, in between, was French. The main ranching areas were in Texas and California, but in the eventual expansion of ranching over the entire West, only Texas cattle were to have marked influence. Spanish in origin, they remained dominantly Spanish until late in the 19th century before the great breeds of cattle imported from the British Isles supplanted them.

When the first English-speaking colonists arrived in Texas, in 1821, they found the southern and eastern areas sprinkled with wild cattle and wild horses. (The Texas plains still belonged to the buffaloes.) For about one and a third centuries the ancestors of these animals had been escaping from Spanish herds. Except in timbered areas the land had almost a solid turf of grass and was watered sufficiently for the hardy stock. As there were no fences, the only barriers against the straying off of animals were men. But white men were few and they were constantly opposed by Indians. The Indians had learned to ride Spanish horses. And the more horses they had, the more they took from ranchers. They preferred buffalo meat to cow meat and did not molest cattle much.

The estrayed cattle and their increase were called "mustang" cattle. Later they were called mavericks. They were unbranded and were as wild as the deer. Nobody owned them. They were considered game animals, like deer, antelopes, and buffaloes. Frontiersmen often hunted them with rifles. They could scent a man as far as a buck deer can. They would not mix with the milk cows of the Texas settlers, for these cows carried man scent. Sharp-horned, strong and exceedingly agile, the wild bulls were dangerous. A wounded bull would often charge the man who had shot him. Occasionally one would charge a man who had not seen him. Even if captured and taken to pens, the calves of these mustang cattle were difficult to domesticate. The stock had reverted to the wildness of the original wild ox hunted by primitive man in those unrecorded times when the dog was still a wolf.

By no means were all the Spanish cattle in the country "mustang." In eastern Texas around Nacogdoches, all up and down the San Antonio

River, and along the Rio Grande from Laredo to its mouth, vaqueros tended—or half-tended—to herds owned by Spanish-speaking rancheros. Many of the branded cattle were as wild as the unbranded. The offspring of branded cows were constantly adding themselves to the far-spread mavericks.

The English-speaking colonizers of Texas were nearly all country-reared and were familiar with cattle. David Crockett, who died in the Alamo, tells in his autobiography of following a drove of cattle afoot for four hundred miles across the mountains of Tennessee into Virginia. But ranching as practiced by the Spaniards was new to these people. In adopting it, they followed the pattern of Spanish ranchers. Some had brought horses and milk stock with them. They acquired Spanish cattle and there was some crossing between their own stock and Spanish stock, but range cattle remained predominantly Spanish. The saying was that it cost less to raise a cow than a chicken.

These settlers were usually good horsemen, but they were not used to bucking horses. They knew nothing of the use of the lasso, or of hunting wild cattle in brush. Not one of them had ever seen a roundup—the original rodeo—on the prairie. Just as they acquired cow horses and cows from Span-

*Texas cowboys were influenced by the
Mexican vaquero*

ish rancheros, they acquired the artifacts and techniques of ranching. They took over from Mexican vaqueros the reata and lassoing, a saddle with a horn to tie a rope to, big spurs, leather or rawhide leggings (chaps), and perhaps the broad-brimmed hat. The Texas cowboy who was to trail longhorns up the Chisholm Trail was in equipment and methods a blend of American, Spanish, and Mexican.

3

Longhorns

Climate, grasses, minerals in the soil, latitude and other factors of nature inevitably made their mark on Spanish stock introduced into Texas. It was further marked by some crossing with cattle brought from the United States. Also, English-speaking ranchers were more selective than Spanish-speaking ranchers in bulls left on the range to breed. By the time Texas was admitted as a state to the Union, the Texas longhorns were generally bigger animals and had longer, heavier horns than the Spanish cattle below the Rio Grande.

Never was a cow brute better adapted to the demands of nature than these longhorns. They could horn off the fiercest wolf, smell out the most cunning panther. When they were driven westward, longhorn bulls did not hesitate to engage with grizzly bears. Their worst enemies were screwworms; longhorn cows licked them out of their calves.

A longhorn did not grow meat on its carcass clean down to the hock, like the Hereford and other man-developed breeds, but the longhorn had "cow sense" to a supreme degree. A cow would hide her newly born calf in grass as cunningly as a doe hides her fawn, leaving it there while she grazed and went to water. She and a dozen or so other cows with calves would band together, two or three of them staying to guard the calves while the others went to drink, those on guard leaving for water as soon as they were relieved. It is the nature of little calves to lie down a great deal of the time; they cannot stay on their feet and travel like older cattle. During a very cold winter in North Dakota, a cowman saw an old Texas cow walking her young calf up and down a draw in which it had been born;

Longhorns did not hesitate to engage with grizzlies

she seemed to know by instinct that its feet would freeze if she allowed it to lie down.

Like all other cattle, the longhorns required water, but they sometimes went for months on very little, getting it mostly in the form of prickly pear, which they chewed through thorns to eat. During drouthy times in the arid Southwest, hardier longhorns, especially old steers, used to graze out as far as twenty-five miles from water, coming in to drink maybe not more than twice a week. (Grass is always shorter, from constant grazing, near water than away from it.)

An old-time cowboy of the trans-Pecos country told me that during one drouth when there was no vegetation near water—that was before ranchmen had dug wells and scraped out reservoirs—he once followed a bunch of Texas steers ten miles out from a spring before they halted to snatch a mouthful of grass. He said that they went in a long walk all the way without once pausing. There is not in the United States today a herd of improved cattle that could or would pioneer with such hardihood.

The longhorns were long-legged, long-backed, and long-tailed. They were not only good walkers individually, but adapted themselves to herd movement. Low-built, short-legged cattle of highly improved breeds could never have trailed thousands of miles across deserts, mountains, and rivers as did the longhorns. Their hoofs were as hard as their horns. They were built for their times; and when the time came to ride to market instead of walking, the longhorn was bred out of existence.

It is to be remembered always that the native home of the longhorn was not the high plains but the thickets and prairies of the southern half of Texas. His instincts were all for the freedom of the wilds. He did not want to leave his native coverts. Here his horns were often ringed with age and as rough as bark—before he was captured to be driven north. Many cattle stayed hidden in brush by day like the deer, coming out to graze on the prairies only at night. No cow work was more exciting than waylaying them and roping them at night. On some ranges, the cow hunters kept dogs to help find and catch the wild cattle.

Cattle too wild and cunning to be caught by man were called outlaws. Their outlawry consisted of the passion and the ability to remain free. A ranchman named Roberts down in the brush country of lower Texas once captured a steer bearing a brand that had been discarded for twenty-five years. That means that the steer must have been at least twenty-six years old. During a quarter century he had been seen only a few times.

Roberts had a waterhole fenced in. Beside the gap entering the pen was a densely foliaged live oak tree. One day Roberts stationed himself in this tree to trap outlaws. After the big steer came into sight through the brush it was an hour before he got up to the gap. Then he smelled along the entire length of each of the ten gap poles lying on the ground. Then he smelled up and down each of the gap posts. No hand had touched them. Then he stepped inside. Immediately he whirled, and for five minutes or more stood facing the brush he had emerged from, motionless, watching. Thirst made him only more suspicious, more alert to danger. As is the nature of cattle and deer, he did not look up. After he at last walked to the water and then whirled for another look behind him before drinking, Roberts dropped from the tree and reached for a pole to close the gap.

Instantly the outlaw was racing toward him. Roberts stood his ground. At a distance of ten feet the outlaw halted and began pawing the ground. Then he moved off, and Roberts barred the gap. Before he was tied down the steer broke several ropes and it took all hands to secure him.

He was killed on the ranch. It would have been useless to try to drive him out.

Many wild cattle could not be held even after they were caught. One way to deal with them was to neck two together, or else neck one to a gentle ox. Another way was to tie the head down to a forefoot. Still another was to cut the knee tendon; an animal so "doctored" could walk but could not run. A method sometimes employed to keep "snaky" cows from running off was to sew up their eyelids. Thus temporarily blinded, they followed other cattle, depending on them for guidance. By the time the thread rotted and they could see again, they were gentle enough to stay in a herd—often in the middle of it, as far away as possible from the surrounding riders. Handling such cattle without pens or fences was labor for twenty-four hours a day.

Many an outlaw achieved more than a local reputation. A brindle steer branded Nine R withstood for nine years all attempts to dislodge him from the rough country about the headwaters of Devil's River in southwest Texas. He had escaped various roundups, had been tied down a half dozen times, and had even been driven three or four times to the shipping pens at Colorado City, a hundred and fifty miles away, only to escape and return to his lair. In 1892 his owner sold out, and John Custer, who had been a trail boss, took a "cow crowd" to clean up the range. The bets were that "Old Nine R" would never be prodded over the gangplank into a cattle car.

But Custer captured him. On the trail to Colorado City he tied him every night, and when the gates at the shipping pens were finally closed, a great yell from the spectators went up. Word had gone ahead that the Nine R brindle was coming, and over fifty men were assembled to see him.

"Old Nine R is going to roll this time," they said.

"Wait," said Custer.

A freight engine pulled a car up against the loading chute, and with other steers Nine R was crowded in. The "bull board" was fastened, the door was pinned shut.

"Old Nine R is gone now," a cowboy yelled.

"Wait," said Custer.

Presently, while another car was being loaded, Custer heard a commotion ahead. He looked. Nine R was racing across the prairie back toward Devil's River. He had somehow by hooking and kicking knocked the door down and jumped out. Custer mounted his horse, took after him, roped him, led him back, put him in another car, and tied him short in a corner.

"Now you can say," Custer announced, "that Old Nine R is safe."

Nine R's liberty, for which he had fought so fiercely, was at an end.

4

Millions of Cattle and No Market

Land is made valuable by population and, apart from the minerals it may contain, by population only. After Texas gained her independence from Mexico in 1836 and became a republic, she had tens of millions of acres without settlers. One man got a whole section for a horse. Cattle were so plentiful and money was so scarce that promissory notes guaranteeing payment of a cow and calf passed for ten-dollar bills.

The only outlet for Texas beef was at New

Orleans, and it was limited. The small herds driven there during the 1830s, succeeded by others during the next few decades, began the trail movement from Texas.

The movement was extended following the war between the United States and Mexico (1846-1848). Cowmen and traders began trailing herds, usually small, into Missouri. According to the best figures obtainable, about 65,000 Texas cattle were marketed in Kansas City in the years 1857 and 1858, along with half that many from Missouri, Arkansas, and the Cherokee Nation (in what is now Oklahoma). Some Texas cattle were driven into Illinois and Iowa, a few all the way to Chicago and then shipped to New York. The trade was restricted by a disease in northern cattle attributed to the Texas longhorns. Then the Civil War put a stop to trail driving.

Discovery of gold in California resulted in such a rush of population to that state and such a demand for beef that several herds of Texas cattle were trailed across the continent to the new mining country. The number of animals involved was not significant, but trailing to California was the real thing.

In the spring of 1854 Michael Erskine of Guadalupe County started for California with about 900 big steers, in addition to nineteen yokes of oxen to pull his wagons. He had only twelve cow hands, but twenty-three men hungry for California gold were willing to help the outfit fight its way. The entire escort was under the command of a frontiersman noted for his vigor and skill in fighting Mexicans and Indians. His pay was $1,500. He got the cattle through, with losses and additions, in about four months. Some Texas drovers had to spend so much time resting their depleted herds at oases of water and grass that they took two, and even three, years to make the round trip. Drouth, desert, alkali water, canyon gorges and foot-cutting rocks and sand were harder to overcome than Comanches and Apaches.

During the Civil War, Texas—one of the Confederate states—was not able to supply the Confederacy with much more beef than it had sent to California. The Mississippi River, held by Yankees, was the great bar to herd movement. While Confederate soldiers in Virginia ate parched corn, Texas longhorns went on increasing and multiplying. When the war ended in 1865, Texas had more cattle than it had ever had—perhaps 6,000,000 head. There is no telling how many of them were ownerless, brandless mavericks, as wild as mountain goats, but there must have been well over a million. On many ranges, with most of the able-bodied men away on war duty, there had been little cow work for four years.

The population of Texas at this time was around 700,000 people. As in other defeated Southern states, the government was broke and most of the citizens were broke. Fully a third of the state on the western side had not been surveyed and did not have a house on it. That land still belonged to the Indians and the buffaloes. Not until 1876 was a ranch established on the free grass of the Staked Plains in the Texas Panhandle. Through the 1860s grown cattle sold as low as a dollar a head. A peddler who went over the country trading one ordinary clock for four cows with calves collected a herd of four hundred animals from people who had no money.

This illustration of conditions could be multiplied many times. A few months before the Civil War ended, twenty families in Goliad County got a herd of about 200 steers together and sent them under a trusted man to Mexico. The family of George W. Saunders, which had furnished twenty steers, received in exchange a sack of coffee, two sets of knives and forks, two pairs of spurs, two bridle bits and two fancy hackamores

The Civil War kept many of the ranges inactive

(headstalls). They had been boiling parched bran, parched acorns, toasted okra pods and other substitutes for coffee and using wooden sticks for knives and forks. Some families got tobacco, flour, and peloncillos (Mexican brown sugar in cones) in trade for their cattle.

The victorious northern states went into a boom as soon as the war ended. Their cattle population had gone down. Their millions of people demanded more beef and had money to buy it. In Texas to the south the cattle population had increased. Here were millions of cattle, few people to consume them, and almost no money. For hun-

dreds of miles between supply and demand lay
land very sparsely settled and wholly unfenced.
No railroad connected the two areas, but the
long-legged Texas cattle could furnish their own
transportation.

Trail driving northward began early in 1866
with something of a rush, but most of the drovers
that year met disaster. In the first place, they had
no assured, definite market place to drive to. After
years of battles, blockades, and lack of communi-
cation, the northern states were to most of them
a foreign country. Some aimed for Baxter Springs
in the southeastern corner of Kansas, near the
Arkansas and Oklahoma boundaries; some for
Sedalia, Springfield, and other towns in Missouri.
Many, in pointing their herds northward, were,
like the boll-weevil in the song, "just hunting for
a home"—a home for their cattle. They were not
hunting grass to graze on; their world was full of
grass, all free. They were hunting people with
money to buy cattle.

Looking back now, it seems as if they were
hunting trouble. As a result of drives into Missouri and Kansas before the Civil War, a strong
prejudice had developed against Texas cattle. They
seemed to carry what was variously called Texas
fever, Spanish fever, splenetic fever. The cattle

themselves seemed not to be sick, but after they had passed through a region in warm weather, the short-horned native cattle grazing on the grass there sometimes took a fever and died. It was supposed that the Texas, or Spanish, cattle communicated the disease through slobber, through dung, or in some other manner.

As was discovered after trail driving had become history, the cattle did not transmit a disease. They carried fever ticks, which cannot survive severe cold. These bloodsuckers carried north in warm weather by Texas cattle would, after filling up with blood, drop off their carriers and lay eggs. The newly hatched ticks then crawled up on grass, weeds, and bushes, waiting for a "host" to come along. When they bit into a bovine "host" they infected it.

In 1855 Missouri had passed a law against the entry of Texas cattle, and Kansas had soon followed with a similar law. The laws had not been enforced, but they were still on the books when Texans tried to drive into those states the year after the Civil War ended. Guerrilla warfare had brought ruin to many citizens along the border between these two states and cast a wide region into lawlessness.

On their scattered, unfocused drives of 1866,

the Texans rode right into the guerrilla country. Desperadoes used the laws against Texas cattle as a disguise for robbery. They stampeded herds at night in order to steal the scattered cattle or to collect bounties for their recovery. Mobs held up drovers, demanding cash for a safe conduct through the country. Few Texans had any cash, and all of them were against paying tribute for what they considered a natural right to go where they pleased. There were killings on both sides, but the Texans were at a disadvantage. They had to deal with mobs in a foreign territory and their herds were an impediment to free movement.

A mob of Kansas Jayhawkers (guerrillas) held up James M. Daugherty, killed one of his men, stampeded his herd, lashed him to a tree with his own rope and, after whipping him, turned him loose with orders to ride straight for Texas. He rode in that direction, but when out of sight he turned west the way the cattle had run. He struck their trail and followed it into a camp his cowboys had made. They had the herd under control but had lost 150 head. By driving at night and finally getting guidance from a buyer who knew the country, Daugherty sold out at a good profit.

One drover who was held up at the Kansas line said, "We'll just drive around this little state."

He drove west until he was well past all settlements and then, dodging Indians and buffalo herds, circled into Iowa, where he readily disposed of his cattle.

Thousands of cattle were sold at a sacrifice, thousands lost to bandits. Some owners held their herds over in the Indian Territory until the next spring. An established market and an established way to reach it were desperately needed.

That market and that way were at hand. The name of Joseph G. McCoy will always be associated with the first cow town in Kansas.

5

McCoy Establishes a Cattle Market

In the spring of 1867 the tracks of the Kansas Pacific Railroad had been laid west to Salina, Kansas. Also, the state of Kansas had so amended its law against the entry of Texas cattle as to permit their being driven west of the more settled areas.

Living near Springfield, Illinois, at this time was a farmer, cattle-feeder, and trader in livestock named Joseph G. McCoy. He was thirty years old, fairly well educated, energetic, and eager to expand his business of shipping cattle to markets. One day he bought some longhorns from a man who had driven them from Texas to Illinois the year preceding. From this man he got a conception of the immense numbers of cattle in Texas without a market. He was on fire with the idea of establishing that market.

It had to be west of the settlements. It had to be accessible to a trail—a trail not yet existing. It had to be surrounded by vast spreads of grass on which cattle by the tens of thousands could thrive while the owners waited for satisfactory prices.

To select a site for stockyards, McCoy made a trip over the new Kansas Pacific Railroad. After viewing Junction, Abilene, Solomon, and Salina, he settled on Abilene. With him, decision meant action. He bought a tract of land joining the townsite and arranged with the railroad company to lay sidetracks. The railroad officials were indifferent. Not a soul among the dozen or two inhabitants of Abilene had any conception of McCoy's dream. He had to build. He had to let drovers from Texas know about this new market. He had to convince feeders and other buyers in the corn belt—Illinois, Iowa, and parts of Missouri, Kansas and Nebraska—that they would find bargains in cattle in Abilene.

Abilene—where was it? What was it? It had been named for an obscure kingdom extant before Christ was born and casually mentioned in the Bible. Abilene, Kansas, was even more obscure and fully as remote. Its most prominent business-man raised prairie dogs in the middle of the village and trapped them to sell as curiosities. He had plenty of spare time. Abilene, Kansas, was a wide place without streets along Mud Creek on the Overland Stage route—a wagon road that had never been graded and that had now been sup-planted by the railroad. Below it the Smoky Hill River valley and all the surrounding country lay carpeted with free grass "as rich as cowyards."

The first Texans who made for Abilene knew only that it was located somewhere toward the North Star. If they struck iron rails east of it, they could follow west; if west of it, follow east. They were moving their herds from grass, through grass, to more grass—a continent of grass surveyed and titled only in spots and wholly un-enclosed.

While constructing stockyards, installing scales, and putting up a hotel that became famous under

Joseph G. McCoy decided on Abilene, Kansas,

the name of Drovers' Cottage, McCoy sent a
scout south to hunt up and trail down every strag-
gling herd possible and inform the owners that
Abilene, Kansas, was the outlet for their cattle.
In McCoy's own words, every herd north of Red
River "was straggling, for they had not where to

as the most likely site for his stockyards

go." The scout rode far down into the Indian
Territory, south of the Arkansas River, and cut
east. The trail men listened to him skeptically,
with suspicion. As ex-Confederates, they put no
trust in any word from Kansas—but they had to
go somewhere.

The first Texas herd to reach the promised market found it by accident; it was bound for California. The market opened late in the season, but about 35,000 head of cattle reached Abilene that year—a fraction of numbers to come.

The next year McCoy sent circulars advertising Abilene to Texas newspapers, which printed them. He had a crew survey a straight route from Abilene south to Wichita, Kansas, and throw up mounds of earth to mark it. This made the northern end of the trail straighter and shorter. While he was attracting cattle from the south, young men he sent out traveled by train east and west to spread word that Abilene had bargains in cattle.

For a time buyers remained scarcer than cattle. Then McCoy thought up an attention-getter. He would exhibit a carload of buffalo bulls where people would talk and newspapers take notice. A California rancher-trader was in Abilene with a herd of horses driven east by vaqueros. Plenty of Texas cowboys were herding cattle on the surrounding prairies. McCoy engaged three vaqueros and four Texans to rope the needed buffaloes. He had carpenters reinforce two stock cars with heavy timbers. The buffalo ropers loaded themselves, their horses and camping equipment into the cars and were pulled west by a steam engine forty or fifty miles to a siding on Fossil Creek.

After locating a small bunch of buffaloes, they maneuvered it as near the railroad track as possible. Buffaloes cannot be driven like cattle, but the riders managed to get several bunches, one at a time, within half a mile of the tracks. Two men would rope one bull by the half-head. The bull would invariably try to fight. One roper would run forward toward the tracks, the bull chasing him, while the second roper followed with slack rope. When the bull turned to fight the man behind, the other would tighten the rope to hold him back. Finally, when the ropers had worked their captive to a standstill, one roped him by the hind legs and stretched him out.

He was left tied down on the prairie until a handcar on iron wheels was pulled by a rope fastened to a saddlehorn to where the buffalo lay. The handcar was provided with a wooden slide, or platform. Men on horseback dragged the buffalo up this slide until he was on the handcar. Then the handcar was pulled across the prairie to the railroad track, on which it wheeled easily to the waiting stock car. There the buffalo had to be dragged up by pulleys, over a bigger platform, into the car.

Tubs of water and hay were placed in the car. Some captives would not eat or drink. Of twenty-four bulls dragged into it only twelve lived. (One weighed 2,300 pounds in Chicago.)

Canvas attached to both sides of the buffalo car advertised, in gigantic letters, ABILENE, KANSAS, THE MARKET FOR TEXAS CATTLE. The train to which the car was attached halted at towns and people turned out in throngs to see the great shaggy bulls. Two or three ropers went along with the exhibit, and at St. Louis and Chicago they roped the buffaloes again as a demonstration. Newspapers featured the stunt. Buyers came to Abilene.

The leader of the buffalo ropers, although still a few months short of his twenty-second birthday, was already a seasoned cowman. A cowboy can ride and rope; a cowman knows cows. He knows their instincts, their habits of eating, sleeping, drinking. He knows that yearlings take shorter steps than grown steers. He knows when to "hold down" the leaders of a traveling herd and when to "push up" the drags. He knows about weights and prices. He knows the cow business from hock to brisket. The young cowman who roped buffaloes for McCoy was named Mark Withers, and he was to become one of the outstanding trail drivers and cattlemen of Texas.

During the Civil War he had helped trail a herd of Confederate steers to Shreveport, Louisiana. There he saw steers from preceding herds so poor and worthless for beef that Confederate authorities turned four thousand of them over to Withers' boss to be driven back west to the Brazos River and released to shift for themselves. No doubt some of them were captured as strays a few years later and driven up the trail to Kansas.

In 1867 Mark Withers had gone as a hand with a trail herd to Illinois. Now, in 1868, he was in Kansas with 1,200 big steers. He had left the Lockhart prairies with only 600, most of them raised by the Withers family, though a few had been bought on credit at $8 apiece. In the Indian Territory he had overtaken another herd of about 600 owned by two young men whose horses were given out and whose hands had quit. He had bought these cattle at $8 a head, agreeing to pay for them when he got back to Texas. He did not sign a note, just gave his word.

After locating his herd on good grass and water about twelve miles north of Abilene, Mark Withers decided he no longer needed a full crew of

cowboys. He kept his Negro cook and four hands
to loose-herd the contented steers, and sent four
hands back home. First, however, he bought two
new wagons and broke cow horses to harness—
four horses to each wagon. He told the men to
drive through Arkansas and buy apples enough
to fill the wagons and then to sell the apples in
Texas. They advertised their apples by putting
samples on poles attached to the wagon-beds.
When Mark Withers saw them that fall they
said they'd had good luck selling some apples and
giving away the others to pretty girls.

After he had been to Chicago with the McCoy
buffaloes, Mark Withers was offered $20 apiece
for his $8 steers. He held them till November and
then sold at $28.50 a head. That was making
money. For twenty years Mark Withers drove
herds up the trail. He drove to Ellsworth, Hayes
City, Dodge City, and other cow towns long after
the market at Abilene was closed. He drove into
New Mexico, Nevada, Wyoming, Montana, and
other states. Some years he had a half dozen or so
herds on the trail at the same time—as many as
15,000 cattle. When he began trailing cattle he
could, he said, buy on credit and sell for cash;
at the end he had to buy for cash and sell on
credit. Then he quit.

But back to Abilene, first of all the cow towns. In 1868, 75,000 cattle reached it. The next year the number doubled. In 1870, 300,000 Texas cattle were driven into Kansas, but only 120,000 reached Abilene. Railroads were building; other markets to the south and west were competing for Texas cattle. The country around Abilene was being taken over by men with hoes and plows. The year 1871 was its last year as a market for trail cattle.

Joseph G. McCoy, despite his success in making a market, went bankrupt. His expenses were great and he sued the railroad for not living up to its contract. In 1874 he published one of the most important books pertaining to the range industry: *Historic Sketches of the Cattle Trade of the West and Southwest.* That remains his monument—that and the history of his activities in establishing a market at the end of the trail from Texas. Some people have said it should have been called the McCoy Trail. How it came to be called the Chisholm Trail is another chapter.

6

Chisholm's Trail

Herds headed for unknown Abilene in 1867 crossed Red River at Red River Station, north by west from Fort Worth, and then kept on north over the trackless prairies until they struck the Cimarron River in the vicinity of what is now Dover, Oklahoma.

Here they came upon a north-to-south line of wagon tracks. Iron wheels and the hoofs of teams had beat down the grass as plainly as if a mowing machine had cut a path through it. In that wilderness of grass the tracks must have been as astonishing to the trail drivers as the print of a human foot was to Robinson Crusoe on his desert island. There was nobody but the barking prairie dogs and the silent little burrowing owls at the mouths of the prairie dog holes to tell them who had made the tracks. They followed them on toward the North Star—and Abilene.

In time they learned that an Indian trader named Chisholm had made the tracks, and they called the route the Chisholm Trail. It led to Chisholm's trading post on Chisholm Creek, soon afterward to be the site of the city of Wichita, Kansas. From this trading post the trail drivers still had to snail across seas of trackless grass a hundred miles and more before they struck the Kansas Pacific railroad tracks—and reached the pinpoint called Abilene. Most of the drivers had never seen a railroad or a steam engine.

They had followed Chisholm's wagon tracks only about a hundred and fifty miles, but within a short time the entire trail from southern Texas to Abilene and then to other points in eastern Kansas was called the Chisholm Trail. On the southern end many prongs fed into it, for herds to go up it were gathered from Wild Horse Prairie west of Brownsville to the salt grass marshes east of Galveston Bay. The Chisholm Trail had prongs in Kansas also.

There it was often referred to as the Texas Trail. Most Texans said merely that they were "going up the Trail" or had been "up the Trail." "The Trail" meant but one trail—the great cattle trail from south to north—just as, at that time, "the war" meant but one war—the Civil War. Within a few years after the trail was established, population had pushed it so far west that it crossed Red River at Doan's Crossing hundreds of miles above old Red River Station, whence it led to Dodge City, Kansas, "cowboy capital of the world," and then clear on up through Montana to the prairies of Alberta in western Canada. This was the Western Trail, sometimes called also the Dodge City Trail. More cattle went up it than up the original trail, but in popular conception the Chisholm Trail stands for all cattle trails over which the long northbound drives were made.

The name of the Chisholm Trail will live as long as the last story of the last cowboy lives. That south-to-north driveway for herds of longhorn cattle will be remembered as long as American frontiers and the east-to-west Santa Fe Trail for commerce and the longer Oregon Trail for emi-

grants are remembered. It is Chisholm's passport
to history.

> *Come along, boys, and listen to my tale;*
> *I'll tell you what happened on the old Chisholm*
>   *Trail.*
>
> *We combed through the thickets and herded on*
>   *open ground;*
> *From that night on it was riding round and*
>   *round.*
>
> *The wind commenced to blow, the rain began to*
>   *fall;*
> *Hit looked, by grabs, like we was going to lose*
>   *'em all.*
>
> *It's sowbelly for breakfast and beans every day;*
> *I'd as soon be a-eating prairie hay.*

This Chisholm of cowboy song and cattle trail
is not to be confused, as he often has been, with
John Chisum, a Texas cowman who drove herds
west into New Mexico, controlled ranges for a
hundred miles up and down the Pecos River, had
an earmark called the Jinglebob and a brand called
the Fence Rail, and became the chief supplier of
stolen cattle for Billy the Kid and his gang. John

CATTLE
TRAILS

CHISHOLM
WESTERN
NORTHERN
GOODNIGHT-LOVING

Chisum had no connection with Jesse Chisholm and had nothing whatsoever to do with the Chisholm Trail.

Jesse Chisholm was born in Tennessee in 1805. His father was a Scot, his mother a Cherokee. The family moved west with other Cherokees and Jesse Chisholm became a noted guide and a trader not only among his own people but with the Comanches and other Plains Indians. He knew the languages of various tribes and could talk in sign language; he served as interpreter at times for army men.

He was never a cattleman. During the Civil War he remained loyal to the Union, moved north from the slaveholding Civilized Tribes, and established a trading post at what is now Wichita, Kansas. Here Wichita Indians and other tribesmen from the south had camped. The year the war ended, Jesse Chisholm loaded his wagons with goods and went down into his old trading country. He followed a route that had been traveled by Indians and an army detachment several years before. He established a trading post on the Washita River, not a great distance from Fort Arbuckle. Here he died in 1868, less than a year after Abilene became a cattle market. He had never seen Abilene, nor had he ever driven any cattle, excepting oxen yoked to a wagon, over the trail that took his name. It is doubtful if he was aware that the name Chisholm Trail was coming into use.

The cattle that were trailed out of Texas before the Civil War and for several years afterward were mainly beef cattle, to supply meat markets. Along in the 1870s it became customary to hold Texas steers on northern ranges for a year or two before they were marketed. The reason for this was that the northern grasses made mature longhorns fatter and heavier. Meanwhile, vast areas that had been occupied by buffaloes were being turned into ranches and stocked with cows and heifers to raise calves. From their earliest entrance into the range of the buffaloes, English-speaking Americans slaughtered these animals with a wastefulness beyond that of any wolf or other predatory animal. Bridging the continent with railroads and cornering the Plains Indians into reservations resulted in mass slaughter of the buffaloes. Box cars that carried goods to Colorado, Montana, and California came back east loaded with buffalo hides. After no buffaloes were left to skin, mountains of buffalo bones were loaded onto east-bound freight trains to be ground into fertilizer.

By the end of the 1870s the Great Plains had

The Chisholm Trail was named for Jesse Chisholm

been vacated by America's great grass-eaters. The buffaloes had been all but exterminated.

For the Indians of the West, buffaloes supplied not only food but raiment, shelter, and tools as well. Their way of life was based on the buffalo. Annihilation of the buffaloes brought them to their knees. Within an astonishingly short time after mass slaughter of the buffaloes began, a continental expanse of grassland lay vacant for cattle and white men.

When the Chisholm Trail opened in 1867 not a cow had as yet been turned loose to graze on the plains of the Texas Panhandle. It was not until 1876 that Charles Goodnight drove thousands of buffaloes out of the wide Palo Duro

Canyon and turned 1,700 cattle loose in a pasture walled by nature—the first ranch on the Staked Plains of Texas. It soon occupied hundreds of thousands of acres. For about ten years the cattle business boomed as it had never boomed. Foreign investors and American capitalists who had never had anything to do with cattle stocked ranches to be managed by cowmen. Texas cattle were planted on newly established ranches in Oklahoma, Kansas, Nebraska, the Dakotas, Wyoming, Montana, the plains of western Canada, parts of Idaho, Utah, Arizona, New Mexico, and nearly every other western state.

The Chisholm Trail and its successors became canals of cattle flowing from the vast breeding grounds of Texas to vast breeding and maturing grounds north and west. According to some estimates, during the quarter century following the close of the Civil War, 10,000,000 head of long-horns went over the trails. That estimate may be high, but the effect of the drives on range history can hardly be exaggerated. It has been said that "civilization follows the plow." West and north of the Missouri River the plow followed Texas longhorns driven by Texas cowboys riding Spanish horses.

These cattle trails must not be thought of as

narrow roads. In places the serried trails spread out several hundred yards wide, one narrow trail closely paralleling another. Usually the cattle traveled eight, ten, maybe fifteen miles a day, depending on waterings. Some of the time they just grazed north. Even when they traveled, they moseyed along at the rate of two miles an hour. They were "thrown off" the beaten trails to graze and to bed down. In a few places, and in a few places only, can the scars of the great trails be seen today. Mostly they have been plowed under or washed away.

Let us picture a herd on the trail.

7

A Trail Herd and Its Management

The Hollywood idea seems to be that any trail herd worth sneezing at should contain at least 10,000 cattle. "What was the biggest herd you ever helped drive?" somebody asked an old-timer who had been listening to talk by drug store cowboys.

"I don't exactly know," he said. "It was so big that by the time the tail end of the herd left the bed ground in the morning the lead cattle were bedding down for that night."

A cowman sending several herds a season up the trail usually put around 2,500 head to the herd, though some put more. Anybody who has worked with cattle knows that a thousand head makes a big herd. There were more little herds than big ones; there have always been more little ranchers than big ones.

Another Hollywood idea seems to be that a trail herd did nothing but run from the Rio Grande to Montana and that the cowboys with it did nothing but run after the cattle, yell, shoot six-shooters, and look tense. Any cowman's idea of handling a herd was to keep it quiet and contented so that when it arrived at its destination hundreds of miles away the cattle would be in better condition than when they started traveling. "When cattle run, they run off tallow." That old saying was based on the fact that fat cattle make money and poor cattle lose money for the owner. The way for the owner to thrive was for the cattle to thrive. They throve on plenty of water, grass and sleep and no lost motion in traveling. A northbound herd was so directed that while grazing the cattle moved slowly northward. When it was time to travel they merely walked on the way they were headed.

A stampede was something out of the ordinary. It was an experience that young cowboys wanted and old ones dreaded. It was something like a fire, which all people rush to behold but no responsible person wants to have happen.

A stampede in which cattle ran over bluffs and piled up in gullies, breaking legs, knocking off horns, and even killing each other, was costly. The great majority of stampedes occurred at night. Occasionally in darkness some cattle cut off from the main body of runners and were lost beyond recovery. A herd crazed by fear might, even after being held up repeatedly, keep running all night long. It would take days for such runners to recover lost flesh.

Sometimes, cowmen claimed, some old rounder in a herd of steers got the rest into the habit of stampeding. Runs of this kind were not usually long or very harmful. One evening John Chisum, who was cowman all through, rode over the bed ground of a herd that had been stampeding every night for weeks. He finally halted his horse near a lanky, one-eyed, corkscrew-horned paint steer about as narrow across the forehead as a razorback hog.

"There's your stampeder," John Chisum said.

"Drive him down to the river and shoot him."

The steer was shot and the herd stopped stampeding.

There were many causes of stampedes. A skunk might whisk the nose of a sleeping steer with his tail. That steer would jump to his feet with a start. All the other steers would jump at the same time, and in an instant the whole herd would be running in terror. Or it might be that cattle used to the odor of white men smelled an Indian. Any unfamiliar sight, sound or smell might touch off a stampede, especially if the cattle were nervous from being tired, thirsty or hungry.

No careful cowboy on herd at night would dismount near the cattle. The reason for this was that his horse, by shaking the empty saddle and rattling leather and stirrups, could start a run. If a cowboy lit a match, he had to protect both flash and flame with his body or hands so that no animal caught a glint of the light.

The cattle seemed to sense that their guards were protectors. Singing to them in the darkness not only kept them aware of their guardians but dimmed out other noises. Cowboys were not, however, picked on account of their voices. Some men had an indefinably soothing effect on the longhorns, just as some people by their very presence and tone of voice soothe nervous horses—and other people.

The master of a trail herd not only kept cattle from running but held down cowboys who wanted to run. He and all hands whom he trusted knew that stampeding cattle could not be halted dead in their tracks by a man riding in front of the plunging column. The object was to circle the leaders so that they would come around into the rear runners, on the inside of the circle. Thus, still following the leaders, the whole herd would be wound into a standstill, the leaders helplessly enclosed in the center. This was called milling. About two good men were usually more effective at bringing a stampede into a mill than fifty yelling, hardriding cowboys could be.

A mill

A typical herd of 2,500 cattle would be driven by about ten men, including the boss. Each would have six or eight horses to be ridden in rotation.

A special hand, the horse wrangler, had charge of the remuda—the horses. A cook drove the wagon. Thus, the boss, the cowboys, the horse wrangler, and the cook made up an outfit.

The boss selected two experienced men to point or direct the herd. They were called pointers or point men. One rode on the right forward corner, or point, of the herd; the other rode opposite him on the left. They were graduates in the school of cow psychology. They knew how to check or veer the lead cattle without stopping them or turning them back. They set the rate of motion as well as direction for a herd strung out a mile, even two miles, long, crawling along like some giant snake over hill and dale. The pointers never excited the cattle; they directed them as easily as they directed their own mounts.

Strung behind the point men at long intervals were the flankers, or swing men. A flank man had several hundred yards of the long thin line to guard. He pushed in any cattle that tended to walk off or stop to graze along his segment of the herd. While passing through timber and crossing streams, he had to be especially vigilant. He rode back and forth except on ground that permitted a clear view in both directions, at a time when all cattle in his sector were moving steadily.

The herd would crawl along quietly over hill and dale

Behind the herd was the drag man. Sometimes there were two drag men. This was not an exciting position, but only a trusted, experienced hand was assigned to it. The tired, the poor, the sorefooted, the lazy, the "loggy," and the obstinately gentle cattle brought up the rear. With herds of yearlings and of cows with calves, often the hardest work of all was to keep them moving. It was easy in broken or brushy country to let one drop behind.

After cattle got "trail broke"—accustomed to staying together both day and night and to traveling and grazing in unison—they usually kept their relative positions in the herd. A lead steer might walk at the head of a herd for a thousand miles, his position unchallenged, the same cattle right at his tail day after day. Charles Goodnight of the famous JA ranch in the Panhandle of Texas had a lead steer named Old Blue that he sent with trail herds to Dodge City year after year. After a herd was delivered, Old Blue would come back south with the remuda. He was a pet and ate all the bread and scraps of food that the cook and cowboys would give him.

The boss had no fixed position with the herd. In the morning he usually rode forward to reconnoiter for water, grazing grounds, camp site; he would watch out for other herds and, if he was honest, would scare range cattle out of the way so that they would not get into his herd. When the going was hard with the drags, he worked at the rear.

In buffalo country he would be on the lookout for buffaloes, which sometimes stampeded herds and enveloped numbers of cattle in their masses. Imagine the freshness and the lushness of the land in wild life before the white man took it over! On the prairies between the Red Fork and the Salt Fork of the Arkansas River in 1871 a cowboy who helped hold one of the Choate and Bennet herds while a vast column of buffaloes passed saw deer, antelopes, wolves, wild horses, and a few cattle moving with them.

In 1875, Ike Pryor, who a few years later had fifteen herds of 3,000 head each on the trail, set out with a herd for Colorado. After the trail crossed Red River out of Texas into the Indian Territory, it ran due north 300 miles to Dodge City. There cattle bound for Colorado turned west up the Arkansas River. When Pryor got across Red River, he decided to cut for Colorado in a northwesterly direction, instead of making the Dodge City elbow. He calculated that this route would save about a hundred miles of travel.

He had never been over the country but knew that it was fairly well watered, and he was willing to take a chance on Indians. There was no trail to follow. While Pryor was scouting ahead on the third day after taking this course, he met two men riding east.

After greetings, Pryor told them that he had a herd behind him and asked them about the lay of the land.

"You'll never get to Colorado with a herd this way," one said.

"Why?"

"Buffaloes. There are millions of them. Nobody could drive a herd of cattle through them."

Pryor thanked the strangers for their information and rode on into the sea of grass. That night the herd was bedded down by fine water, and it snored in peace till daylight.

The next afternoon while Pryor was scouting some distance ahead of the oncoming herd, the cook following him in the wagon, he saw something that made him halt.

"What is that dark cloud on the horizon away ahead there?" he asked the cook.

The cook had no opinion. It was soon apparent that the cloud was coming toward them; then that it was buffaloes. The front of the herd was

The boss would see that the herd was well settled

wider than the eye could compass; there was no break in the oncoming column, and seemingly no end.

Pryor galloped back to the herd, telling the cook to follow. As he approached the point men, he gave the sign to halt. While the drag cattle were still coming up, the wagon was halted and the horse wrangler brought up the remuda. After catching fresh mounts, the men roped all the other horses and picketed them to a long rope that encircled the wagon. The cattle were halted so as to enclose the wagon and horses.

After telling off six men to hold them, Pryor

rushed forward with six other men to meet the buffaloes. They met about half a mile from the herd. By yelling, shooting, beating with quirts on their leather leggings and waving slickers, the riders managed to split the herd, so that half passed to one side of the cattle and half to the other.

All night long the buffaloes rumbled by. All hands stayed in the saddle working at the double job of keeping the buffaloes spread out and the cattle held in. At daylight next morning buffaloes were still passing, though the tail end of the herd, about a thousand drags, was in sight. Ike Pryor made no guess as to the number of buffaloes that had passed, but he knew there were hundreds of thousands, and he did not want to risk encountering more of them. He pointed his herd back to the Dodge City Trail.

A good boss considered the welfare of his hands and horses as well as of his cattle. In drouth, heat, and winds, he would rotate the positions of his men every day or half-day so that those on the dustier side of the herd were relieved. I know of one trail driver whose eyesight was permanently ruined by constant irritation from herd dust. The fresh flowers of springtime were not always blooming on the trail. A common practice was to tie a handkerchief folded trianglewise over the nose so that the down-hanging flap shut some of the dust off from mouth and nostrils.

Nowhere was the boss more watchful than at waterings. Ideally, the herd would graze into water and across it, but if cattle were very thirsty they would crowd into it and many be ready to leave before the drags and the more timid animals had a chance to drink. The boss saw that the herd stayed on water until the last animal had drunk. Some animals would not drink unless they had plenty of space and time; some nervous-natured animals would not drink if a horseman was moving near.

A boss who knew his business would see that a herd grazed over the ground they were to bed down on, thus becoming familiar with it and less likely to scare in the night. Trail cattle seemed to prefer bedding down on a gently sloping hillside. The boss regarded this preference. He saw that the herd had plenty of room to lie down in, and that it was not too closely bunched. Often he stayed with the herd through the first relief to see that it was well settled and to detect any signs of nervousness.

The boss of a trail herd, cut off alone for months with his cattle and men, had the responsibilities for

life and property that the captain of a sailing ship
on the high seas had. He was supreme commander,
but he managed his men without being bossy, just
as he kept his herd under control in such a way
that the cattle would not feel restrained and con-
fined. He had to be ready to meet both the expected and the unexpected.

The experiences of certain trail bosses will il-
lustrate.

8

Indians and a Desperado Sash

One of the main ranch families of old-time Texas was the Slaughters. When he was eighteen years old, William B. Slaughter, long since dead, bossed a herd of 2,000 steers on the trail for Abilene, Kansas. They belonged to his father, who was a Baptist preacher as well as a cowman.

Somewhere in the Indian Territory, the Slaughter outfit met a crew of cowboys riding south mighty fast. They said Indians had taken their herd.

Billie Slaughter did not propose to turn back, but when he was an old man he said he felt more shaky that evening than at any other time of his life. His father had picked a very religious cook named Porter to go up the trail with his son. As soon as camp was made, young Slaughter asked Porter what he thought about going on. "Will we get through?" he asked.

"Well," Porter replied, "I'll have to talk to the Lord about this."

After supper Porter went away out to one side, built up a little fire, and by the light of it read his Bible. Then he prayed.

The next morning before daylight while Slaughter was pouring coffee out of the coffee pot into his tin cup and nobody else was near the campfire, the cook announced: "We'll get through all right."

"How do you know?"

"The Lord told me so. I've talked to Him and He has talked to me. No need to worry now."

The herd moved on that day and made camp for the night without trouble, but Slaughter unceasingly expected it. An idea for meeting it developed in his mind. Not long after midnight, he mounted his night horse, already saddled, and rode out to where a seasoned trail hand named

Wash Wolf was standing guard. It was a beautiful night and the cattle were all bedded down and breathing heavily in sleep. Slaughter knew that Wash was a hard character. He was from South Texas and had been in some kind of "difficulty." But he was the best hand in the outfit, and before the outfit started up the trail Parson Slaughter had made him promise to see his boy through.

When Bill Slaughter rode up to him, he did not appear a bit glad to see him.

"Billie," he said, "what are you doing out here this time of night?"

"I want to see you and talk with you," the young boss replied.

"Well," Wash Wolf went on, "can't you trust me?"

"Yes, I trust you fully."

"Well, the cattle are all asleep and the night is fair, and there's no trouble stirring. You don't think I'd go to sleep on herd, do you?"

"No, I don't think you'd go to sleep on herd."

"Well, what *do* you think?"

"Give me a little time, Wash, and I'll explain. You know the Indians are out ahead of us and we're bound to meet up with them soon. You are quick to fight, but we've got to get these cattle through without a fight and a stampede, no matter what we have to stand from those Indians. You promised my father to see me through. Now I want you to promise me that you will not shoot until I give the word."

"Well, I don't propose to be run over by any Indian on earth, but I'll promise."

"All right, Wash. Now I want that desperado rag you keep around your waist."

Wash Wolf wore a red Mexican sash about six feet long and three wide. "Billie," he said, "if you knew the story of that desperado rag, you would not ask me for it. I'll tell you how I got it when we get to Abilene. I just wish you wouldn't ask me for it."

"If you'll let me have it, when we get to Abilene I'll have Colonel C. C. Slaughter buy you a new suit of clothes."

"I'd give half a dozen sashes for a new suit of clothes," said Wash, and he took the sash off and gave it to his boss.

"I have a plan," Billie said, and went back to camp and to sleep. The next morning when he started the herd on north, he carried Wash Wolf's desperado rag and three new red bandana handkerchiefs folded neatly in the bosom of his shirt.

About noon the herd halted on the south side

He waved the bandanas and sash in front of the chief

of Wolf Creek for dinner. Billie Slaughter "sort of smelt Indians." He told the cook to put to one side a good supply of flour, coffee, bacon and sugar. Before the hands were through eating, about thirty Indians rode up. The chief came directly to the wagon and demanded food. He got the supply already arranged for him. Meantime, some of the warriors were whipping the cowboys' horses and the cowboys were following instructions not to start anything.

At this point Slaughter unbuttoned his shirt, pulled out the three big red bandanas and the long desperado sash and waved them in front of the chief. The chief was delighted. He said he wanted beef, and Slaughter had three sore-footed steers cut out for him. He and his followers killed them at once and made camp. The Slaughter outfit drove on for Abilene.

"The Lord told me we'd get through all right," the cook said that night.

Indians usually expected a few head of cattle from any trail herd they met. After all, the country the herds crossed belonged to them.

9

The Biggest Trail Herd

Indians were only one of the obstacles that called out the resources of trail bosses.

Walter Billingsley was born to a trail-driving inheritance. In 1857 an uncle of his, with three other cowmen, gathered 1,200 mossy-horned steers and headed them for Chicago. They swam the Mississippi River about twenty-five miles above St. Louis. Butchers in Chicago contracted for them, stipulating that they be herded on the prairie outside the city limits until needed for beef.

Every day or two the cowboys drove a bunch into a pen and shot them down with sixshooters.

With this tradition behind him, Walter Billingsley, while yet in knee breeches, began working cattle for neighbors in southern Texas. When he was seventeen years old, he launched forth on his own hook and with a brother went into the Mexican country south of the Nueces River to gather cattle that had strayed away from owners living on the north side. The Billingsley brothers got two dollars a head for every animal they brought home. This was in the spring of 1879.

At the age of twenty-two, in the spring of 1884, Walter Billingsley hired as boss to Captain Richard King of the famous Santa Gertrudis Ranch to take a herd up the trail. His pay was $100 per month. His herd consisted of 3,300 two-year-old steers. Under him he had ten hands, besides a cook and remuda man. All but one were Mexicans. On the morning of the first day of April he strung the herd out.

Four other King Ranch herds were going up the trail that spring, each leaving a few days after the preceding one. They were all under the supervision of Henry Stevens, who went ahead to Dodge City. Each trail boss, crossing nearly a thousand miles of country, was for about three months solely responsible for a herd of cattle valued at around $50,000. Every animal in the five herds was branded **K** on the left jaw and ∿ (Running W) on the left side.

Young cattle are more fractious than mature ones, and Billingsley's two-year-olds started running the first night out. For sixty hours he was out of the saddle only long enough to change horses and snatch a few bites of food. Gradually the cattle became used to trailing and being under herd.

Every animal in the five herds was branded

North of Pease River, Billingsley found grass so good and water so plentiful that he decided to lay over a while for his men to rest and the cattle and horses to mend. For ten days the young steers did nothing but graze and water at leisure and sleep quietly on their bed grounds. And then they were strung out again. They passed Doan's Store, just south of Red River, where cowboys in love asked for mail and posted letters.

Trailing through the Indian Territory was a pleasure. No stampedes, no Indians, plenty of water and grass. It was a good year. About the first of July Billingsley halted his herd on Mulberry Creek, twelve miles south of Dodge City, and rode into town to report to Henry Stevens. That night he saw a bad man called Mysterious Dave kill Bing Choate, a south Texas cowman, in a gambling row.

After the herd had been held on Mulberry a week or more, Henry Stevens told Billingsley that all five of the King Ranch herds were now in and that he was in a tight spot. The trail boss of one herd was quitting, or had been fired, and his remuda of horses was in such bad condition that nobody wanted to ride them, and no trail man of good judgment was willing to take the respon-

sibility of handling a herd on them. Stevens pro-
posed to cut a thousand big steers out of this herd
and turn the remainder, all two-year-olds, over
to Billingsley to combine with the cattle he already
had. They were all contracted for delivery on Hat
Creek in Montana.

"I already had the limit in numbers," Walter
Billingsley said. "A herd of 4,000 is enormous.
A herd of 5,000 is simply too big to water out
properly. Some won't get water or won't get
enough. And here I was to have more than 5,000.
But there wasn't anything to do but double up,
and I agreed. I had one advantage. All the cattle
were trail broke."

There was a disadvantage too. The Mexican
vaqueros, excellent hands, had gone as far north
as they were willing to go. They turned back for
the Rio Grande, and Billingsley got a new outfit
of cowboys, mixed Texans and Kansans—sixteen
of them now.

All the cowmen in Dodge City rode down to
the Arkansas River to see the great herd cross.
A King Ranch man sitting on his horse on the
north bank counted 5,533 head of two-year-old
steers come up the bank. Old trailers said that
Walter Billingsley would never get through with

such a herd. But he was young and full of confidence. The doubts of others were a spur to his own determination.

The trail led through Ogallala, Nebraska, on the Platte River—another wild and wooly cow town—260 miles north of Dodge City. This part of the trail, however, had been closed to ticky cattle from southern Texas. Two enterprising cowmen, Dick Head and Martin Culver, had somehow got concessions on a route farther west for ticky cattle to travel. They were charging three cents a head for cattle driven over it. Their trail measured 310 miles. It was defined by two parallel furrows, three miles apart. The ground between the furrows belonged to trail men and their cattle, but they must not leave it.

The big drawback to this trail for ticky cattle was not the added distance but the lack of water. There were two fifty-mile stretches without water and one forty-mile stretch. Fifteen miles was considered a long day's travel. Driving a thirsty herd for fifty miles without a drop of water would make any person comprehend how far a mile can be.

The first night north of Dodge City, some of the Texans began to quarrel with some of the Kansans. Farther travel did not add to harmony between the groups, but they drove the cattle on.

Billingsley held the herd on Pawnee River until every animal had a belly full of water. Then began the first of the dry stretches. For thirty miles the trail lay west alongside a new barbed-wire fence—a sign that before long there would be no through trail for cattle. The country was burning up. The plodding herd raised a dust that could have been seen for miles. The massed cattle gave off a furnace-like heat that almost blistered the face of any man riding near it on the leeward side. After a day without water the horses were suffering. The men drank sparingly from a barrel in the chuck wagon.

While the herd was halted for noon rest, Billingsley said to some of his men, "There is water over in that pasture the other side of the fence. I'm going to find it and water our horses. If you see me wave, bring them on."

He let down the wires and rode over them. After riding not more than half a mile he sighted a lake and waved his hat. A half dozen men immediately followed with the remuda. The watered horses were back at the fence about to recross it when a fence-rider appeared.

"Well, I've caught you," he said with as much dryness as the lowing cattle showed. "You know this pasture is private property and not to be trespassed upon."

"Yes, I know," Billingsley answered. "Where are you from?"

"Texas."

"What part?"

"Austin."

"Look here," Billingsley went on. "We are not about to drive that big herd of cattle into your pasture. These Texas horses simply have to have water. We're not damaging you."

The fence-rider relented enough to allow the men on herd to water their horses. Then the barbed wire was restapled to the posts and the thirsty herd, tongues out and lowing, moved on.

After following the fence west for thirty miles, the trail veered due north. By now some of the steers merely moaned instead of lowing. Their eyes were shriveled back deep into their heads. Darkness came and the herd still trailed on. Along in the night a dry norther blew up. The lead cattle at once lifted their heads and began trotting. As Billingsley afterwards learned, he was about nine miles south of Smoky Hill River when the norther hit. How far cattle can smell water is one of the debated cow country subjects. "I know these smelled it nine miles away," Billingsley said.

The herd was strung out for miles. Racing up one side and down the other, Billingsley ordered all hands to change horses and try to hold the cattle back. The fight had been to keep them going; some would stop and look far away or try to turn back to where they had last watered. Now the fight was to keep them from stampeding and piling up on each other in the river. When the lead steers reached the Smoky there was just one man behind the herd, miles back. That man was the boss. He followed the drags into water about eight o'clock in the morning.

A fill of water and a day of rest and grazing restored the young steers markedly, but they still looked gaunt. They trailed by Fort Wallace, crossed the South Republican, the North Republican, and the Frenchman rivers, went for another fifty miles without water, and then snailed across sandhills to Ogallala on the Platte. Here, so his Texans reported to Billingsley, four of the Kansans "took a freight train." It seemed peculiar that they did not draw their pay before taking it.

While the herd was still in the sandhills, the Montana buyer rode south from Ogallala to inspect the steers. They "looked like gutted snowbirds," he said. He was scared of his contract, said that the cattle were not up to specifications, and got his forfeit money, $25,000, back from Henry Stevens, who had moved up to Ogallala.

Billingsley, after watering the herd on the Platte, moved up-river and went into camp for a rest. Within a week the steers showed wonderful improvement. The manager of the Bay State Cattle Company rode out to look at them and was so well pleased that he bought them for sixteen dollars a head, a dollar more than the Montana buyer's contract called for. They were to be delivered at the head of Horse Creek, 150 miles northwest of Cheyenne.

While the herd was on bed ground a few miles out from Fort Sidney, Nebraska, the boss gave men not on herd permission to go to town and see the sights. Five failed to report for work next morning. Billingsley rode to town, found them, and fired them. He owed them $120 apiece, had no money, and did not know a soul in Sidney.

"My first move," as he used to tell this part of his story, with gusto, "was to see the banker. I explained to him that I was trail boss for the famous King Ranch and had fired five men to whom I owed six hundred dollars. Would he cash a King Ranch check for that amount?

" 'Well,' the banker said, 'you look all right and I am satisfied you are all right, but can't you get somebody to identify you?'

" 'I'm where I never was before and where I never expect to be again,' I replied. 'I don't know a soul in this town.'

"The banker seemed anxious to accommodate

He asked the banker to cash a King Ranch check
for $600

me. 'Suppose you look around a little and see if you can't strike somebody you know,' he concluded, 'and then come back.'

"I went out. I had a plan. I rounded up the men I had fired and said, 'Follow me and get your money.'

"We galloped to camp. 'Load up and hitch up,' I said to the cook, 'and follow me.'

"Then I called the horse wrangler. 'Drive up your remuda,' I said to him, 'and follow the chuck wagon.'

"When we were all ready, we struck a high trot for town, and a sight we must have made!—I in the lead, the five cowboys who had been fired on account of their faithlessness swinging after me, then the chuck wagon with six mules hitched to it, and then a hundred and fifty saddle horses with the horse wrangler and two other hands driving them. I drew up in front of the bank, and the outfit halted. So did traffic.

" 'Come here,' I yelled to the banker, who was already at the door. 'Come out here and look at my identification.'

"He came, laughing.

" 'Now,' I said, 'I guess you know what the King Ranch brand is—Running W on the side and K on the jaw. Well, there are a hundred and fifty saddle horses branded K W. There's a wagon with K W branded on the side-boards and chuck box. Look at the cook's saddle on the mule he's riding, and you'll see K W on it. In fact, everything and everybody in this outfit is branded K W.'

"The banker was impressed, all right. Without another word he cashed the check. The quitters unsaddled their horses right there in the street and turned them loose with the remuda. Then the Running W outfit rolled on for Cheyenne."

At the head of Horse Creek, Wyoming, the manager of the Bay State Cattle Company and Walter Billingsley counted the steers as they strung between them. They agreed on the count—5,533 head—the tally made on the north bank of the Arkansas River, two months and 800 miles away. After helping brand the steers and taking a last look at them as he left them grazing, Billingsley rode with horses and wagon back to Ogallala, where he had instructions to deliver them.

As he was about to take the train for Texas, he met John T. Lytle, one of the best known operators from Texas. He said he was holding a herd of 3,500 steers that had to be driven to the Belle

Fourche, six hundred miles away, and needed a trail boss. He offered Billingsley $175 a month to take charge of the herd.

"I thanked him kindly," Walter Billingsley related. "The wages offered were a compliment, but I had had six months and five days of trail dust and I was through. I would not have gone on the trail again that day for a thousand dollars a month. I had shaved, taken a bath, put on a new suit of clothes, and was headed south. We were already sleeping under two blankets up there, and I foresaw that a drive to the Belle Fourche would be an ice-breaker. Anyway, when a Texas cowboy rolled his tail and went to sniffing for the Gulf breeze, he was drifting south. You could no more stop him with an offer of good wages than you could stop a wedge of migrating geese by sticking a telegraph pole in front of them. I made other drives and have followed cows through every thicket in southwest Texas, but driving those two King Ranch herds in one was the most memorable experience I ever had on the trail."

10

The Cook and His Chuck Wagon

At the time of the Civil War there was not a chuck
wagon in Texas. For years after the war ended,
men out on cow hunts carried their own grub in
a wallet tied behind the saddle. It consisted of
bread, salt bacon, salt, and coffee. Sugar was still
a luxury; vegetables and fruits in camp were unknown; indeed, they were uncommon in ranch
homes.

Meat could be killed when needed. Some of it
was usually jerked, or dried. Fresh meat was spitted

over the coals on sharpened green sticks driven into the ground. Bacon, always salt pork, was broiled on the end of a forked stick. Many an early-day range hand drank his coffee out of the can in which he boiled it. He carried his bed—a blanket—under his saddle. If the weather got cold he could keep the campfire burning all night. If he ran out of bread and had some flour, he mixed it with water, wrapped the dough around a stick, and held it over the fire until it was ready to eat.

On the earliest trail drives from Texas into Louisiana, a pack horse or pack mule carried provisions for the crew of drivers, along with the few necessary cooking utensils. One man might be delegated to look after this pack animal and cook.

When the longer drives northward began, a trail outfit usually took along a cart. Oftener than not, it was pulled by oxen. In addition to carrying food with pots and pans, it carried light bedding.

The first wagons on the trail did not have built-in chuck boxes, but they had plenty of room for iron pots containing cooked beans. Beans for supper had to be cooked the preceding night. In time, chuck wagons carried cases of canned goods, though cowmen from lower Texas never spent much money on such luxuries. A wagon had room for ample bedding and some extra clothes.

Under the wagon bed was slung a dried cowhide, called possum belly or cooney (from the Spanish word *cuna*, cradle), for carrying fuel. When the wagon left timbered country for the plains, the cooney was filled with wood; when wood ran out, it carried cow chips or buffalo chips.

The cook was an institution. There were mean cooks and kind cooks, clean cooks and dirty cooks, good cooks and poor cooks. Whether a cook liked the cowboys in his outfit or not, he cooked for them, no matter what obstacles he had to overcome to make a fire.

At times when water covered the ground on which camp had to be made, the cook would shovel up a pile of mud so that he could build his fire on it, above water level. Absence of water was more often a handicap than its presence. Out in the dry Pecos country a wagon boss once said to his cook, "Scour your pots with sand and wipe 'em with a rag."

"Rags all used up," the cook replied, "but grass'll do."

Whether on range or trail, the cook was supposed to be cranky. Cranky or not, the cowboys had to get along with him. The most obliging cook stood apart from them.

The cook was usually older. Often he was of another nationality or color—Negro, Mexican, or German—in contrast to the Anglo-American blood of the great majority of trail men. While they were enjoying their only social hour of the day, which was brief, after supper, he was washing dishes, peeling potatoes, and making other preparations for before-daylight breakfast. As he worked alone, he slept alone—under the wagon, often the only shade for a nap and the only roof against rain or sleet. This space was his sanctuary, and his bed there was inviolable. Although he was just a pot-rustler among men on horseback, he drew from five to twenty-five dollars a month more than they. Yet a proud spur-wearer would no more take the cook's job than descend to sheepherding. In fact, the spur-wearers often put sheepherders and cooks in the same category.

The cook had no authority beyond his chuck wagon, but for sixty feet around it—the length of the longest roping rope—his authority was supreme. If he did not maintain it, his work was demoralized and the whole outfit became demoral-

Around his chuck wagon the cook ruled supreme

ized. No man was supposed to ride his horse into that kitchen area or otherwise stir up dust near the food. No man, unless the boss was excepted, could tie his horse to a wagon wheel. Not even the boss had license to take food until the cook announced that it was ready.

In the popular conception of range men their home background is ruled out, as if they had been born full-grown among cows and had never known a gentle mother, sat at a family table, and heard the blessing asked. One of those who never lost his background was a man named Frank Smith; and if there ever was a professional trail cook, it was he.

After running away from home in the "auld country" as a boy, Frank began cooking for railroad gangs in California. He saved his money and bought teams that he hired out for construction work, at the same time cooking for the drivers. He liked to cook. He had cooked in Montana before he arrived in Austin, Texas, and went out on the William Blocker ranch, where he took over a kitchen superintended by one of the finest ladies ever revered by cowboys. In this kitchen he would allow no one to touch his flour can or coffee can. No "cowboy coffee" for him. He scoured that coffee pot after each meal. He would cook for cow hunts and drives and, after range work was over, cook for the family.

Bill Blocker and John Blocker were for a time partners in trail herds; later John operated alone. At the height of his operations he had over 80,000 head of cattle on the trail in one season. The first year Frank Smith went up the trail he loaned John Blocker $4,000 at interest. At the same time he was drawing $60 a month, which was $15 more than the average cook drew and twice the amount paid trail hands.

One day while the Blockers and the Shaw boys were preparing to go up the trail, Mrs. Bill Blocker got Frank Smith to help her cook fruit cakes. She said to him, "Can you keep a secret?"

"Yes, ma'am."

"Well, I'm giving you two fruit cakes and two bottles of wine to take along. Save them until they'll really be appreciated."

The longhorns snailed along by day and sometimes stampeded by night. They had crossed Red River and were away up in the Indian Territory when the coldest, wettest, blowingest spring weather that a cowboy ever shivered against came and persisted. The bed rolls were all wet. One evening when John Blocker came into camp, he remarked, "I don't know what I'd give for a real meal with cake and all and something to cheer me up."

"How would you like to put your feet under Mrs. Blocker's table tonight?" Frank Smith asked.

"I'd sell out for a big slice of her fruit cake right now," John Blocker replied.

"I'll give you two slices of her fruit cake," Frank Smith went on without cracking a smile. He wasn't much of a smile-cracker anyhow.

"Yes, and I'll cut your throat with a butcher knife if you go on tantalizing me," John Blocker retorted.

About this time Frank Smith unwrapped a cake and poured a bottle of wine into tin cups. That was one treat of fruit cake and wine in camp that none of the hands ever forgot.

Ab Blocker for many years bossed herds and ranches for his brother John—"Brother Johnnie," as Ab called him. He never owned anything and never wanted to own anything, but he modestly agreed with other range men from the Rio Grande to the Canadian line that he was just about the best trail boss that ever delivered a Texas herd on the Yellowstone. He claimed that he had looked down the backs of more cows and drunk more water out of cow tracks than any other man who ever pointed a herd toward the North Star. Many times I have listened to his stories. Always he put more emphasis on Frank Smith than on any other individual he associated with on the trail.

One of the first things Frank Smith did after he went with the Blockers was to build a chuck box. Up to that time he had not seen one in Texas. His was devoid of the compartments common in later chuck boxes. It was square and bolted to the bottom of the wagon at the rear end, the exposed side hinged so that it could be let down to serve as a table. Everything in the wagon was in order. At the left front end was a 45-gallon barrel for water; against it at the right front end was bacon, often 500 or 600 pounds. Then came flour and other provisions, and stacked between them and the snug chuck box (filled with stores for immediate use) were the outfit's personal belongings.

Preparatory to serving a meal, Frank Smith would place tin plates, cups, knives and forks in a circle. Then, pots and pans of food in front of him, he would stand in the center of the circle. Thus, waiting on the men himself, he saw that each got a fair portion. There was none of the wild grabbing and spooning for choice portions common in some camps; men coming off herd to eat after the others had eaten got as well fed as the first ones served. Morning and night, Frank

Smith had hot bread, but for lunch—a hasty meal —cold bread had to do. He pitched the bread around to the hands from his position over the Dutch oven, and if any man took more than he wanted to eat, that man stood a good chance of having to eat the remainder at the next meal. Frank was saving of everything, but of bread especially. When through eating, the men, one by one, deposited their utensils on the chuck-box table.

Sourdough, common on the plains, was unknown in the original cow country and is still little used in that part of Texas. The sourdough cook—called a "sour dough" himself—had a jar or keg holding up to five gallons in which he made a batter of flour, salt and warm water— nothing else. He kept it warm for a day or two —in the sun, by the fire, even in bed with himself—until the contents fermented. This was his yeast. To make bread he mixed some of the yeast with flour, soda, salt, lard, and water. After taking a portion of the fermented batter out of the keg, he regularly added more flour, water, and salt. Thus the base for bread was kept for months —maybe a year or more—until the keg or jar had a dried crust around it an inch or so thick. Only then need it, like an over-crusted pipe, be cleaned out.

Bread in the original longhorn country was made with baking powder added to flour or meal, along with water, salt and grease—generally lard but often melted beef tallow.

Camp bread, whether made with baking powder or sourdough, is cooked in a Dutch oven—a big iron skillet with short iron legs—set on coals with other coals heaped on the lid, the pones thus cooking evenly from both above and below.

Frank Smith had a recipe for making yeast that he kept secret. It was known to include Irish potatoes. He carried it in a two-gallon lidded bucket and swore that a cup of it placed in a box of sawdust would make the sawdust rise. The men who ate his pones, as light as lightbread, were willing to believe him.

His pastry was equally delicious, pies from dried apples being his specialty. Sometimes pie would be left over. This he kept for the last relief on herd.

"Many a time," Ab Blocker said, "I have asked him for a piece of pie that I knew was in the chuck box."

"I'll see you in Jericho before I let you have

it," would be Smith's invariable reply. "Those hard-working devils standing last guard are the ones that are going to get this pie."

Cowboys new to the outfit would sometimes complain to Ab Blocker that they could not get along with "that cranky old cook."

"Just wait," Ab Blocker would reply. "Before long you'll be stealing wood for him."

Sure enough, the complainers would soon be stealing wood and doing everything else they could for Frank Smith. They learned to appreciate his fairness, even if he always sided with the boss in any difference. He was loyalty itself to his outfit and, while hospitable to strangers, fed his own men before giving any food away.

11

Remuda and Remuda Man

Before trail driving became a rather conventionalized procedure, little outfits drove their spare saddle horses along with the cattle, hobbling them at night. In time a horse wrangler became as customary as a cook. He was sometimes called the nighthawk.

Often, particularly on cow works, the wrangler was a boy. Any boy wanted to be running and roping instead of poking along all day with a bunch of gentle horses, letting them graze and keeping them from scattering, and then staying out with them at night. For many a "button," or boy, taking care of the horses was a step in his education toward becoming a top hand.

On the plains and over all northern ranges the bunch of saddle horses came to be called cavy-yard or cavy—a corruption of the Spanish word *caballada*. The word properly denotes a band of stock horses—mares and colts with a stallion. In southwest Texas that meaning is preserved, and remuda is the only term used for a bunch of saddle horses. There also remudero is the name for the man who takes care of the remuda.

A good remudero, or wrangler, knew horses, liked horses, wanted to be with horses, and had ways of controlling them unknown to many expert cow hands. He was kind of kin to horses. Sometimes he was an oldish man who did not want to tear around.

What a shepherd dog is to a shepherd in keeping a flock of sheep together and driving them, a bell mare was to a remudero in grazing and driving his horses. This remuda mare wore a bell, and horses associated with her came to respond almost involuntarily to its tinkle-tinkle. The bell on a grazing animal makes an irregular, halting tinkle compared with what it makes when the animal is traveling. When the bell mare, urged by the wrangler, stopped grazing or maybe woke up from standing asleep and took out, you could see the scattered cow horses switch their tails in a kind of harmony with the clinking bell and start following it. The majority of them would have stayed with the remuda mare even if she wore no bell, for most horses like the company of a mare.

The "mother mare," as called by the Mexicans, was often selected on account of her gray or white color, so that she could be better seen in darkness. For this very reason of visibility, frontiersmen during Indian times avoided riding light-colored horses.

A good wrangler never close-herded his remuda, for horses naturally scatter out while grazing, and it was highly important that they eat plenty and keep strong. Each cowboy had from six to ten horses in his mount. He rotated them regularly, and if the wrangler saw that the loose horses grazed freely, he would ordinarily at the end of months of work and travel have the animals in first-class condition. Of course, the way a cowboy rode had a great deal to do with his horse's condition. Some cowboys were so hard on horses that they could not hold a job.

A good remudero knew horses and liked to be with them

A good wrangler knew every horse in a remuda, maybe fifty, maybe a hundred head. When he drove them up in the morning for fresh mounts to be roped out, he might say, "Well, I see I'm short three head. One of them is that P O dun. Another is Pico Blanco (Snip Nose). He always runs with that white-footed black in Waddy Hone's mount." After the horses to be ridden that morning had been caught, the wrangler would leave the others grazing while he hunted the three missing ones. Knowing the nature of the country and of horses, he would set out for a certain spread of land. If he did not find them pretty soon, he would "cut for sign"—look for the trail they had made and follow it. If they had walked on grass coated with dew, the trail was easy to follow. Whether it was easy or hard to follow, the wrangler was expected to bring in the strays and have the entire remuda at the noon camp a few miles up the trail for change of mounts.

There were no pens on the trail to put the horses in. When fresh mounts were to be caught, several cowboys standing in a circle made a temporary pen. Each, acting as a post, held a stretched-out rope about waist high. While a horse was being broken he learned better than to try to run over a rope. A big remuda of cow horses would stay inside this one-strand rope fence. One man, usually the boss, roped out the horses, each cowboy calling out the name or description of the horse he wanted.

Negroes and Mexicans often made outstanding remuderos. There was Alec Gross, a Negro, who went up the trail under Ab Blocker time and time again. He was old enough to be white-headed, and everybody called him Uncle Alec.

After he had been out a week with a remuda,

he would have the horses following him instead
of his driving them. He always carried a whip,
but did not often punish a horse. He simply had a
way with horses. If he looked back and saw a horse
stopped for any reason, he would point his whip
handle at the horse and call out, "Hep, hey, come
right on up here." The horse would usually start
in a run and not stop until he was at the head of
the remuda, right behind Uncle Alec.

Alec Gross did not drive his horses into the
rope corral, but led them into it, with a power
akin to that employed by Indian Buffalo hunters
in leading a herd of buffaloes to an ambush. "Hep,
hey, come in here together," he would shout, and
the horses would follow him into the rope circle.
After mounts had been caught, he would again
shout, "Hep, hey, git out o' here and go to grazing," and they would go off to one side and begin
mowing grass.

Uncle Alec was an expert roper. If somebody
missed a throw at a horse, he would say, "Jes' let
your old Uncle Alec ketch him." Then he would
throw his loop with a twang as if he meant to cut
the head off the wanted horse. That horse might
be in the middle of the remuda with his head
down, seemingly protected by the bodies of other

horses. No matter, Uncle Alec's loop would en-
circle the target.

He wanted no help. If the chuck wagon had
stopped, the herd just beyond it quietly grazing,
and some cowboy rode out to help Uncle Alec
bring the horses up, he would say, "No, sah, I
doan need no help. Please go on to camps and
unsaddle yoah horse and lay down and rest a little.
Please doan help me none."

He always hobbled his horses at night and
wanted no help in this business, either. He would
take a handful of hobbles and crawl in among
the horses and hobble them without having to
rope one. The meanest and most skittish horses
in the remuda would allow him to put hobbles
on their feet.

Alec Gross was a horse man by both nature
and training. He was the wonder of all trail men
who observed his ways as remudero.

Just as outstanding was Teofilo Hernandez,
a Mexican remudero who worked under John
Rigby, a noted boss. His bell mare was an old
dun who had two or three grown-up colts in the
remuda. They followed her, but not any closer
than the other horses. She was a fighter and would
often back her ears and kick horses right and left.

That conduct seemed to make them more eager for her company.

When on the trail, Teofilo led this dun mare, the entire remuda, generally around seventy horses, following. If some horse did not follow well, he would rope that horse, no matter in whose string the horse belonged, and ride him for several days, leading the mare from his back. Generally this close association would make the horse so attached to the mare that he would thereafter keep close to her.

At night Teofilo would take the horses to some grassy patch of prairie land a quarter or half mile from camp, and there stake the mare by a long rope to a stake pin driven into the ground. Then he would ride off to one side, unsaddle, stake out his horse, and lie down to sleep with his saddle for a pillow. About four o'clock in the morning, the boss in camp would hear the dun mare's bell coming. When Teofilo got near, he would dismount, drive a stake pin into the ground and tie the mare up short to it. The remuda would bunch around her, most of them going to sleep. Horses seem to do their soundest sleeping just before daylight.

A remuda trained by Teofilo required no rope pen. The horses in it would stay bunched around the bell mare while being roped out for riding.

The most important horse in a trail driver's mount was the night horse. A good night horse could see unusually well in the dark, was "clear-footed"—did not stumble while running over rough ground in darkness, rain, or lightning—and had superior cow sense. Nearly always he was oldish with lots of experience behind him. Maybe all he did, night after night, was walk for from two to four hours slowly around a herd at peace on the bed ground. He knew as well as a clock could have told him when it was time for the guard to change; then he was likely to try to pull away toward camp. But let the herd stampede, and then he could teach a young cowboy something about the cow business. Life and property depended on him, and he did not fail.

Horses are like people in habits. Some night horses could sleep at any time; some seemed unable to make up for the loss of sleep. This was especially true of night horses on the last guard before dawn. On long drives the guards were rotated, the first "trick" of the night being the easiest and the last the hardest.

Now and then a horse wrangler preferred a mule to ride. It was held by some that mules see better, smell more keenly, and make more wary guards over a remuda than horses.

Whether he was riding a horse or a mule, lying down on the grass, or standing with his chin in the saddle watching the Morning Star, a wrangler who liked his job felt that the horses he lived with, a large part of the time alone, made good company.

An old saying had it that a "horse wrangler that ain't lazy ain't no good." It was made by riders who wanted to plunge through fire and flood. Just the same, when one of them got sick or crippled, it was the horse wrangler who took his place on guard at night. Whether his horses were hobbled or not, he could trust them and the bell mare not to graze far from the ground he located them on in the evening. Not every good cowboy could be a good wrangler, but a first-class wrangler knew how to handle cattle. Many a time he put his horses into high water just ahead of the herd to lead it across a river.

Stampeding cattle sometimes seemed to try to outrun a cold wind from the north. Horses, on the contrary, would hump up with their tails to the cold and stand. They have been known to stand with drooped tails to a blizzard until they were actually frozen to death in their tracks.

In February, 1894, a northbound herd on the Pecos River was struck by a blizzard that brought blinding sand and then sleet. The men managed to hold the herd, but when morning came they could see nothing of horses or horse wrangler. All hands except those with the cattle went out to search.

Along in the afternoon a cowboy found the wrangler with just two horses. According to his story, he became so nearly frozen in the night that he lit a match to a big rat's den amid prickly pear and, after the dry sticks making the den burned up, lay down on the warmed ground and fell asleep. He woke up before long, mounted his horse, and then found his remuda gone. He took out to find them and by daylight was lost. Later he found just two. The others were brought in during the day by scouting cowboys.

At daylight after a stampede, a wise horse wrangler would take the trail of the stampeders and follow it with the saddle horses until he caught up with the exhausted cattle held by tired men on tired-out horses. They might blame him for not getting there sooner, blame him even for the storm, but they were mighty glad to see him.

Like the cook, he was apart from the men who drove the cattle. In many ways he was just as important, for as the saying went in the days of the Horse Age, "A man on foot is no man at all."

12

He Stayed with the Herd

For every boss there were at least ten "just common hands." Some hired for money, and some for fun; some to be going somewhere and some to leave somewhere; some for experience and some to escape experience. Whoever and whatever they were, irrespective of color, age, or position, a good hand stayed with the herd. That was his test.

Staying with the herd denoted a certain amount of endurance. Above that, it denoted pluck, loyalty, trustworthiness, honor. The range had no

higher compliment to pay horse or man than
to call him a "stayer." The stayer "would do to
tie to." He "would do to ride the river with."
The tests came by high water, thirst, cold, hunger,
craving for sleep, stampedes, thieves, hostile In-

A good hand always stayed with the herd

dians. They came also in the daily round of experiences between man and man as well as between
man and nature.

On the first day of March, 1892, an outfit of
L F D cowboys began trailing a herd of three-year-
old steers northeast from their range down in New
Mexico to Amarillo in the Panhandle of Texas.
The winter had been open and seasonable; grass
was already greening. The third evening out, the
northern rim of the sky had a blue-black tinge;
before the second guard came in, a cold norther
was blowing hard; by daylight, the sky was spat-
tering snow. No break in the rolling plains offered
protection. It is against the nature of cattle to
travel against a blizzard, but, urged on by the
never-turn-back men, the L F D steers kept their
northward course.

About sundown, while the cattle were settling
for the night, the wind died down and a drizzling
rain set in; by morning the water was freezing
into icicles on grass and bushes. The cowboys who
wore moustaches had catwhiskers of ice on them.
Sleet, mixed with rain, fell all day, but the cattle
traveled better than the day before, for there was
no cold wind to face.

Then, toward nightfall, the wind rose into a
howler. The cook, an oldish Negro named Jube,

did the best he could, but all he had to make a fire with was wet cowchips, and wet cowchips won't burn well in rainy weather no matter how hard you fan them with your hat. The hungry men understood why their food was only half-cooked; they thanked Jube for boiling-hot coffee. There was no changing of the guard that night. Every man circled the restless herd all night long. The next day, they trailed on. There was no place to take shelter from the wind on those open plains.

When finally the weather moderated and the sun shone, the beds of those L F D hands had not been dry for ten days and nights. The boss let the herd lay over for a day beside a lake while the bedding dried and the men caught up on sleep.

On the third day of clear, mild weather, the herd came in sight of Palo Duro Creek and Jube went to singing old-time plantation songs. He could see scrubby hackberries a long way ahead, and he had promised the boys spice cake—minus the eggs—whenever he got to wood.

That afternoon the rim of the sky to the north took on a blue-gray look, and within an hour a bitterly cold dry norther blotted out the world with driving dust and sand. The riders had to rub sand out of their eyes to see, and the more they rubbed, the more irritated their eyes became. It was a relief, but only momentary, when sleet replaced the sand.

There was no singing on herd that night but there was coughing in all tunes. Every man had a cold down into his chest. Those in camp coughed as hard as those on herd. But Jube had wood to burn, and he boiled sage tea strong enough to scald the lining in a man's mouth, almost, and every man swallowed it. The cattle milled all night long.

Among the men on guard the first half of the night was a youthful Negro named George, the only Negro cowboy in the outfit. He was not warmly clad. A cowboy on guard with him named Mack McAvoy saw how cold George was and heard his spasms of coughing.

"George," he said, "we can hold the cattle without you. They are not going to run, just mill and mill and maybe drift. Go to the wagon and turn your horse loose and cover up."

George's teeth were chattering as he answered, "I can stand it if the rest of you all can."

The two men remained halted a little while near each other, the cattle being temporarily quiet. To quote McAvoy, "Presently I saw George lean over his saddle horn, coughing and sounding as if he were losing his breath. Then he went to the ground. By the time I got to him he was as dead as a mackerel and as stiff as a poker. He had simply frozen to death sitting on his horse."

The next day the L F D men placed George's body in the chuck wagon and drove to the top of the highest rise of land overlooking the Palo Duro. They dug a hole deep enough so that coyotes would not dig the body out. Then they rolled the black cowboy in his blankets so that dirt would not get into his face and covered him up. They left him there on the lone prairie with only a stub of hackberry for a headboard.

There was no inscription on this grave marker. Long since it rotted down and, like many another cowboy's grave, George's is now unknown. Yet in the imagination of those who know, there is a marker there, granite in durability, graved with these words:

HE STAYED WITH THE HERD.

When men grouped together with one purpose, living in one common way, are isolated in prolonged association and work, they develop loyalties of comradeship and fidelities to a common duty. For thousands of years soldiers and seamen have experienced and felt this loyalty of comradeship and duty. A good trail outfit developed the morale and clannishness of Xenophon's army of Greeks retreating through the hostile Persian empire to the Mediterranean. "I wish I could find words," said Charles Goodnight, who was a great man as well as cowman and who broke more cattle trails than any other darer of the open range— "I wish I could find words to express the trueness, the loyalty to their trust and to each other of the old trail hands. I wish I could convey in language the feeling of companionship we had for one another."

Goodnight was of the Southwest. Granville Stuart of the Northwest, sometimes called "the father of Montana," said of the cowboys he worked with: "Their faithfulness and loyalty to their outfit cannot be described. They were to their outfit what a good mother is to her family."

Many hands, of course, failed to fulfill these ideals, but the ones who counted did.

The drives from southern Texas to Kansas and beyond were generally timed to start after grass had begun to green and the severities of winter were past. Yet, however slowly the herds moved northward, they sometimes outdistanced advancing spring and met severe weather. In 1874, Sol West got a particularly early start. His idea was to get to buyers with his big steers ahead of competition. He left the coast country on

February 27 with a dozen cowboys, seventy-eight horses, and an ox-drawn wagon.

Sol was very young to be a boss, coming twenty-one, and hardly a man under him was older. He had already been up the trail three times, which meant that he had matured. The cattle, all grown steers, were his own on a rather unusual contract. His older brother and a partner had agreed to let him have them at a certain price, on credit, he to drive them and sell them and then, after deducting all expenses, to receive half the profits—if there were any.

All went well until the 8th day of April. Sol West had scouted ahead and picked a campsite on Hell Roaring Creek, in the Indian Territory. Misting rain and light snow fell all day with a brisk but not hard wind from the north. About three o'clock in the afternoon, just as the lead cattle came within about a hundred yards of where the wagon had stopped, a blizzard struck. The steers at once turned from it, going back south. All hands combined could not stop them; all they could do was check them. One man was spared to help the horse wrangler hold the remuda.

By dark the herd had drifted about five miles, the thermometer going down and down. Meantime, even under the saddle, the horses were freezing to death. Their blood was too thin for that temperature. When Sol West saw what was happening, he told the dismounted men to go—walk —back to camp. His horse was the last one to go down. Two men were still with him, both afoot. The wind had subsided a little and the cattle had been checked in a pocket of low hills.

Each of the three men had a metal waterproof matchbox with matches in his pocket, but their hands were too numb to get the boxes out, much less to strike a match. Standing there in the darkness, they saw a dim light away off in the hills. They started toward it and after more than an hour of struggling reached a dugout. A man named Jim Taylor, who was not an authentic cowman and who was hiding out with several followers, made the footmen welcome to a warm fire, hearty food, and then pallets with plenty of bedding. The Texans had had nothing to eat since daylight.

Sol West and his two cowboys were up at dawn before anybody else had stirred. He saw a dun horse under a shed back of the dugout, also a saddle. He appropriated both and made for where he had left his herd, the cowboys following on foot. The herd was still there. Soon the other cowboys who had gone to camp the evening before appeared—all on foot.

The two horses ridden by the remuda men and every one of the sixty-five horses in the remuda had frozen to death.

But Sol West on his borrowed dun horse and the other men afoot got the herd moving toward camp. Only well trail-broken cattle could have been managed in this manner. After cattle had been under the direction of men for weeks and were in a land foreign to them, they, even though still wild, often seemed to rely on their drivers.*

Snow, sleet and ice covered the ground eighteen inches deep. Hell Roaring Creek was frozen over solid. About halfway to camp, Sol West saw a man on foot coming in his direction. He proved to be a "trail neighbor," a man who was bringing a herd just behind the West herd. All his horses and work oxen had frozen to death and his cattle were scattered to the four winds.

When the West outfit reached camp, they found Jim Taylor of the dugout and about fifteen other men waiting. Taylor was not pleased over

---

*Late in 1871 Sam Garner of Lockhart, Texas, bossed a herd driven from the Solomon River in Kansas to Salt Lake City. A snowstorm overtook them, covering the grass so that neither horses nor cattle could get to it. Fourteen horses froze to death right in camp and many cattle died. "Old wild beeves," Sam Garner said, "became as gentle as work oxen." For three hundred miles the men drove them afoot.

appropriation of his dun horse. He considered the circumstances, however, and agreed that $1.50 for use of the horse would settle the matter. "I did not tell him," Sol West used to relate, "that there was only ten cents in cash in our whole outfit."

West traded him several steers for three horses and a mule—and the $1.50 owing for use of one dun horse. For two days the herd was held on Hell Roaring Creek with three horses and a mule. Meantime West traded steers to Indians for three more horses. The wagon oxen had survived.

Sol West believed that even if he had not gotten more than a horse or two, those cowboys would have driven the steers to Ellsworth, Kansas, where, some of the men behind them still on foot, they arrived on May 20.

1874 was not a prosperous year for cattlemen. A panic of the preceding year had sent the price of cattle in Kansas down as low as one cent a pound and had broke many cowmen. Cattle in Texas were being slaughtered for their hides and tallow, the meat thrown away for buzzards and coyotes. Although Sol West's herd was the first to reach Ellsworth, it took him the remainder of the year to sell out the steers, a few at a time. It was December before he and his outfit got back to where they could smell the Gulf of

Mexico. When accounts with the furnishers of his steers were settled, he had exactly seventy-five cents as net profit for his year. But he and his men had certainly stayed with the herd.

13

Lightning and High Water

No experience branded itself more deeply into trail drivers' memories than that of electrical storms on the plains. Cowboys from the south were used to lightning, but not this kind. A human being has to be out in the elements at their wildest, reduced to the level of other houseless animals, to comprehend the might, the majesty, and the terror of a storm on the shelterless plains.

John Connor was night-herding the remuda

alone on the prairie, out of sight and sound of camp or herd, when the storm struck. The lightning, overhead and all around, was one continuous, dazzling flash; the thunder roared deeper and deeper, nearer and nearer. John was nineteen years old and considered himself "as brave as any man," but when the horses bunched helplessly around him, stuck their heads between their knees and groaned, he got down and lay flat on the earth. It seemed to him in that hour that "the end of time had come."

Occasionally, for some cowboy, the end of time did come. While Mark Withers, his brother Gus, and a man named Johnson were riding together, about to count out a herd of cattle that had been sold, a bolt of lightning killed Johnson, put out one of Gus's eyes, but only burned the plush off Mark's hat. One night south of Red River, four cowboys out of a crew of eight, driving only six hundred steers, were sitting in camp when a bolt of lightning struck in their midst, killing one and burning the others so badly that one had to quit.

Death from lightning was not frequent, but it was a frequent threat. People in those days had an idea that metal attracts lightning; so they put up lightning rods on their houses and many a cowboy in an electrical storm got rid of his hardware.

George Brock, leading two extra mounts, was riding alone south of the Platte River to meet and pilot a second herd belonging to his boss. "I thought I knew all about Kansas storms," he later related, "but that afternoon I learned I didn't.

"The lightning would strike the ground and set the grass on fire, then the rain would put it out. I got down off my horse and tied him and the other two together, took off my spurs, sixshooter and pocketknife, laid them on the ground, and moved off to one side. Before long the sun was shining and the world looked as if nothing had ever happened to it."

Sometimes it didn't look that way. In July, 1881, as many as fifty herds, it is said, were being held up and down the Arkansas River south of Dodge City, Kansas, waiting on contracts for drives farther north and west or to be shipped east. One night a storm brought all hands to duty.

It may not have been more spectacular than some other storms of the western plains, but its consequences were. The atmosphere was charged with electricity. A man could see it playing along the brim of his hat and on the tips of his horse's ears. Foxfire skipped from horn tip to horn tip over the surging masses of cattle. Sporadically the rain fell in torrents. Now it was dark, and now the welkin was lit up in ghastly brilliance so that thousands of cattle and scores of horsemen were visible to one pair of eyes. There was forked lightning, chain lightning, flash lightning, yellow and red and then blue lightning. An electrified atmosphere smelling of sulphur settled down like a fog. The clack of horns against horns, the rattling of hocks and the pounding of hoofs blended with the rumbling thunder and the terrifying cracking of electrical discharges. One man saw nine big steers knocked dead near him.

"That storm made a cowpuncher long to be at headquarters or in a snug dugout," one of the men said. But the only place to be was with the cattle.

A herd would split. Cowboys would hold up what they could, and then here would rush into them part of another herd. After a while no man could tell which were his cattle and which were not. The next morning all the different outfits got together and made a general roundup over the whole country. It took nearly a week to get the various brands cut out and separated into their original herds.

*In deep water a man's only dependence
was his horse*

Crossing high water was not so noisy as stampedes in a storm, but it could be more dangerous.
Now and then a man was drowned. Among ranch
people of the last century swimming was not
much of a sport and many a cowboy did not
know how to swim. In deep water his only
dependence was his horse. If some horse in his
string had proven himself a good swimmer, he
shifted his saddle to that horse before entering
a high river.

A good river horse was as prized as a cutting horse. In fact, the regular hand, who never cut cattle out of a herd but only held them while others did the cutting, valued a good night horse and a good river horse above all other horses. Not infrequently, the night horse was extra good at swimming. To swim freely a horse must have the girth and the reins loose. Sometimes the bridle was removed, sometimes the saddle also. Saddles could be carried across on a raft improvised out of logs, or in the wagon, which also was often rafted across.

In 1871 W. B. Foster, who was twenty-two years old and fresh into Texas from Illinois and Tennessee, hired to an owner named Todd to help drive a herd of big steers up the trail from the San Antonio country. According to Foster, he and a seventeen-year-old boy were the only members of a crew of twenty-two men—twice the usual number—that "had not killed a man."

He soon learned that the best all-around horse in his mount was a big, powerful black that he named Jack Moore. Just after passing the village of Hillsboro in Texas, the lead steers spied a little girl walking across the prairie to school with a red shawl around her head and shoulders. A high wind was whipping the corners of it above the tall grass. The curious steers started trotting and then running toward the object. Foster raced Jack Moore ahead of them just in time to reach down and pick up the red-shawled child and carry her to safety.

One morning in the Indian Territory he was running Jack Moore after a wild turkey when he rode into a bunch of hostile Indians. Jack Moore carried him swiftly back toward the herd, but both man and horse received several arrows. After they were pulled out of him, Foster had to ride in the wagon a week before he could sit comfortably in the saddle again.

It was at Red River, before this episode, that Foster and Jack Moore saved the herd. For a long distance up and down the river there was only one good crossing. The river was a raging flood, swirling big trees and smaller drift downstream. Nobody wanted to plunge in ahead of the cattle, but they were well strung out, and when the leaders came to the south bank they went right into the water. The other cattle followed. In midstream a floating tree made the leaders circle back, and soon hundreds of animals were in a mill, circling. Milling cattle are free on the outside of the circle, but those toward the center are so pressed against that in deep water they go under.

Todd, the owner, sitting his horse there on the bank, cried out in despair, "Where is Foster? I'll give him anything in the world to save my herd."

Foster jerked off his saddle, pulled off his hat, shoes, shirt, and trousers and, wearing only undershirt and drawers, rode Jack Moore into the maelstrom. He entered upstream from the cattle. At the edge of the circling mass, he picked out a big steer, gave him a scare toward the north bank, leaped from Jack Moore to his back, and rode him across. At the edge of the water he slipped off his back and drifted down to where Jack Moore was coming out. The mill had been broken; the other steers were following the big one that had made it across.

This was about nine o'clock in the morning on the eighth day of June, and the sun was blistering. Hatless, saddleless and riding only in his underclothes, Foster held the herd alone until nearly sundown before the other hands and the wagon got across.

Sometimes the men stripped naked to cross a swollen river. This is what the men with the Nance herd did at the North Canadian in the summer of 1877, but they did not unsaddle their horses. A naked cowboy was across the river with about half the cattle when a violent hailstorm stopped the others from following. There was no timber on the south side of the river, but the north side was heavily timbered. The men on the south side made a run for the wagon and got protection. The man on the north side got under a tree. After the storm was over, the ground was covered with hailstones two inches deep, and the river was higher than ever, the water ice-cold.

The cattle would not take it, and neither man nor horse could endure the cold long enough to cross. At intervals during the remainder of the day several men came near drowning in attempts to carry clothes to their comrade. On account of the timber, they could see nothing of him or the cattle.

The next morning was clear and warm. After a while the man who had spent nearly a day and all night alone with half the herd rode out of the timber and swam back to his clothes and to the first food he had tasted in more than twenty-four hours. In those days saddle pads were not used on the range, only folded blankets that could be used for covering—provided the user did not mind the smell and feel of sweat and horsehair. This man had passed a comfortable night, he said, wrapped in a good saddle blanket. He had seen no sign of Indians and had left the cattle grazing contentedly. Before long the whole outfit was across the river, trailing on for Cheyenne.

14

Comanches on the
Goodnight-Loving Trail

Despite exceptions, Indians encountered on the Chisholm Trail were mostly friendly, and were not so dreaded as the Plains Indians on the Western Trail. All of them, whether on their own reservation land or not, customarily demanded "wohaw"—beef—as toll. What they usually got were strays, sore-footed animals, or something else that the cowmen were not reluctant to spare. Sometimes they stampeded a herd at night; occasionally they killed somebody. After about 1876 the Plains Indians were pretty well under army control, but were still loose in an unoccupied land of immense dimensions.

Bossing a herd from near the Rio Grande up the trail to Dodge City and then on into Wyoming, in 1878, R. J. (Bob) Lauderdale encountered in the Indian Territory a large band of Cheyenne and other Indians who had been brought south against their will and who were now, against army orders, going back north to their Dakota homelands. The warriors said that their squaws and papooses were "heap hungry," and Lauderdale gave them two cows. "I always had a stray or two along," he later explained, "and could afford to keep Indians friendly."

A trail boss who followed him over the same ground the next day refused to give these Indians anything at all, whereupon they rode into his herd and shot down eighteen of his fattest steers. Then they went on the warpath. Three outfits camped in the region turned their herds loose and rode for Dodge City for protection. The only man molested was the cook for one of the outfits. Indians killed him, chopped up his wagon wheels, cut the harness to pieces, and took the horses.

The most peril to life and property was in

When Indians were refused a cow or two,

trying to cross the plains into New Mexico. That way, too, lay the most terrible expanse of desert thirst known to the Texas trail drivers. There was no such exodus of cattle in that direction as to and through Kansas, but it amounted to hundreds of thousands. Ranges of New Mexico, Arizona and Colorado that had never been stocked called

they would sometimes go on the warpath

for longhorns. Denver and other mining centers demanded beef. At the close of the Civil War the army had thousands of Apaches rounded up around Fort Sumner on the Pecos in New Mexico and was buying beef to feed them.

In 1866 Charles Goodnight determined to drive west. This was the year, it is to be remembered,

of the disastrous drives into Missouri before a
dependable market was established at Abilene.
Goodnight was thirty years old and was the per-
sonification of vigor and decisiveness. He had
spent all his life on the frontier and had scouted
the plains, where few white men had yet gone,
against the Comanches.

The Comanches claimed the Staked Plains east
of the Pecos and on up into Kansas as their land
—and for generations they had held it. It was pro-
lific with buffaloes. Here Goodnight had witnessed
a migration of buffaloes that he estimated to be
125 miles long and 25 miles wide. He doubted
that anybody could get a herd through this land
of buffaloes and Comanches. His idea was to skirt
it southward on the east side, cross a waterless
semi-desert west from the Concho to the Pecos,
and then go north up the Pecos to Fort Sumner.
This route was roughly a half circle.

Goodnight's range was in Palo Pinto County,
on the fringe of white settlements to the west of
Fort Worth. Only one other cowman to whom
he explained his plan wanted to dare with him.
That was Oliver Loving, twenty-three years his
senior. Loving had driven a herd to Colorado before the Civil War, sent another to Illinois, and
taken several herds to the Mississippi River.

In June, 1866, they set out with eighteen well-armed cowboys and 2,000 mixed cattle—steers, cows, bulls, young stuff. The cows were having calves, and as a little calf cannot keep up with a traveling herd, every morning calves that had been born during the night were shot and left behind. Mother cows trying to go back to their young naturally made trouble, but Indians did not. The herd went up the Middle Concho to its head-waters and then ninety-six miles without water to Horsehead Crossing on the Pecos.

It took three days and three nights for the herd to cross that stretch. Three hundred perished on the route. The only sleep any man got during the whole time was in cat naps on his horse. This trail came to be called the Goodnight-Loving Trail. For years it was plainly marked by bleached skeletons. On the western side of the dry stretch the frantic cattle sometimes plunged into alkali lakes and then died on the poisoned waters. The only way to avoid that disaster was to regard the wind and to direct the herd so that it would not smell the water.

Two months after setting out, Goodnight and Loving arrived at Fort Sumner. One cowboy had 170 sets of rattles that he had cut off the tails of snakes killed along the way. The owners sold

steers that would not bring $10 in Texas for $80;
Loving trailed the cows on up into Colorado and
sold them at boom prices. The drive had been
free of Indian troubles. Goodnight rushed home
for another herd, traveling only at night and carrying $6,000 in gold and silver coins on a pack mule.

He bought 2,000 big steers at Texas prices, and
repeated the drive. The steers walked out like
oxen and only five died on the waterless stretch.

In the spring of 1867 Goodnight and Loving
set out from Palo Pinto County with two herds.
The most dramatic encounter with Indians in the

*Many cattle perished on the long waterless
stretch*

annals of trail driving was ahead of them. Indian trouble began soon after they left home. Both owners went ahead with the first herd, leaving the second to a competent boss. He lost a thousand cattle to the Comanches. They themselves lost 160 head in a night attack and stampede. Here one of their men received an arrowhead in his neck and Goodnight pulled it out with a pair of nippers. At Horsehead Crossing the Comanches got 300 more cattle.

After the herd had trailed up the Pecos a hundred miles or so, it was decided by the partners that Loving should take one man and ride on ahead to Fort Sumner. It was late in June and government contracts for beef were to be let in July. Loving was to bid on several contracts for supplying army posts in New Mexico and Colorado.

"One-Armed" Bill Wilson was designated as Oliver Loving's escort. True, he had but one arm, but there was no cooler- or clearer-headed man on the Indian-harrowed frontiers. Goodnight advised the two men that, alone as they were, they could get through the country only by riding at night and hiding during daylight.

They rode away into the harsh and habitationless land. The rest of the story came later from their own lips as told to Charles Goodnight, who at the age of ninety told me. It is repeated here mostly in his own words.

Loving and Wilson rode two nights and rested one day without coming upon a single Indian sign. Loving detested night riding and was in a hurry to make contracts. He persuaded Wilson that they were being over-cautious. On the second morning, after making coffee and grazing their horses a while, they struck on up the Pecos. About two o'clock in the afternoon while they were crossing the plain that lies between the Rio Azul (Blue River, now called Black River) and the Pecos, in the southern part of New Mexico, they saw a cloud of mounted warriors approaching from the southwest. They were Comanches—more than 100, maybe as many as 500. The only shelter in reach was the Pecos four miles away. Loving and Wilson headed for it in a long run.

At the point where they hit the river the bank drops abruptly for a hundred feet. Somehow they scrambled down, still on their horses, the Indians hot behind. At the foot of the bluff the two men dismounted, hitched their horses, and hid themselves among the sand dunes and *carrizo* (river cane) brakes between the bluff and the river channel. Some of the Comanches swarmed down the bluff after them and in a few minutes had their horses. But those Comanches knew that the men they had run to ground were well armed, and they hesitated to beat about for them in the tall cane.

Many of the Indians had stopped on the bluff overlooking the scene, and one of them yelled in Spanish for the Texans to come out and consult. Wilson advised Loving to keep a sharp lookout to the rear while he himself advanced to guard the front. A few minutes later a bullet from some Comanche creeping up through pole-cat bushes broke Loving's arm and another bullet wounded him in the side. Wilson hurried back and supported him into some tall weeds that concealed a sandy depression against and into the bluff.

The Indians now knew about where the men were but could not see them or fire directly on them. They wasted many arrows and bullets shooting down from the edge of the bluff. For hours Wilson and Loving hugged the ground. One Indian more daring than the others began creeping toward them, parting the weeds and cane ahead of him with a long spear. Wilson saw the shaking cane and prepared to greet him. He knew that the moment he shot, the whole pack of waiting tribesmen would rush forward. He waited.

Then a giant rattlesnake, disturbed by the advancing spear, began to whir, at the same time sidling toward the concealed men but looking at the Indian. The Indian retreated and the rattlesnake passed unharmed almost over Wilson's leg. Neither Texan moved a muscle.

As the long summer afternoon dragged on, the Indians shot arrows high into the air, trying to aim them so that they would come down at the right place. Then darkness came and unceasing howling from all sides. Loving's wound had produced a high fever and Wilson slipped to the water's edge and got a boot full of water.

About midnight the moon went down. Loving begged Wilson to leave him. He did not want to die, he said, without his family's knowing what had become of him. Wilson, he thought, might get back to the outfit and bring relief. Finally, if he himself was able to stand the Indians off, he would wait for help two miles down the river.

At last Wilson yielded. Loving had a Henry rifle that shot metallic cartridges and this he gave to Wilson. Wilson turned over his own six-shooting rifle to Loving and placed around him their five pistols, all loaded. Then with a hand clasp he said goodbye. At the edge of the water he took off his shoes and stripped off all his clothing except underwear and hat and hid them. How with one arm he expected to swim—for swim he must—and carry the rifle, one cannot imagine. A hundred yards below him was a shoal on which he saw a mounted Indian standing guard.

Three times he tried to swim with the gun. It nearly drowned him. Then he punched the muzzle of it down in the sandy bed of the river and leaned the butt against the bank under the water. He now got under some smart weeds and drifted silently down the current. As he neared the Indian on the shoal he saw him splashing the water with his foot, just playing. At last, when he considered himself safe from observation, he made for the east bank and began to travel. He traveled many miles before he recrossed to the west side of the river.

He was barefooted and everything in that country has thorns on it—mesquites, catclaws, a dozen kinds of cactus. At first he traveled only at night. Then he went by day. He picked up the small end of a tepee pole and used it for a walking stick. He went for three nights and into the third day without a bite to eat, without seeing a sign of a human being. The last night out, as he told the story, the wolves followed him from dusk to daylight. He would "give out like a horse" and lie down in the trail and drop off to sleep, and awake with the wolves all around him, snapping and snarling. He would knock about with his stick, go on a way, the wolves dogging his tracks. He was keeping right down the Goodnight-Loving Trail, and about noon of the third day he came to a cave that he had noticed on the last trip up.

Wilson's brother and Goodnight were pointing the herd some distance down the trail from this cave when they sighted the lone man. At first they took him for an Indian, and Goodnight ordered the herd shaped for a fight while he galloped forward to a hill for reconnaissance. When he got within a quarter of a mile of the cave, the lone man gave him the frontier sign to come to him. He stood between Goodnight and the declining sun. His underwear was saturated with red sediment from the river and he made a strange and awesome sight standing there on the barren rocks. Yet somehow Goodnight recognized him.

He was so broken and starved and so shocked from realizing that he was saved that at first he could tell nothing. His feet were swollen beyond all imagination. Goodnight put him on his horse and carried him to the wagon. There men wrapped his feet in wet blankets and fed him gruel. After a while he related what had happened.

As soon as fresh horses could be saddled, Good-

night took all hands except barely enough to hold
the herd and rode for the place where Wilson had
left Loving. It was fully sixty miles away and
every man believed that Loving was dead. Late
next day the party arrived and found Wilson's
gun and pants and even a pocketknife hidden, just
as he had described. But there was no trace of
Loving. They searched all down the river for miles
without finding a sign. At last they concluded that
after killing Loving and scalping him the Indians
had thrown his body into the river. The only thing
left to do was to return to the herd and bring it on.

Two weeks later a cowman met on the trail
gave Goodnight the startling news that Loving
was at Fort Sumner, New Mexico. Goodnight
rode forward at once and reached his "old pardner" in time to hear the rest of the story. The
Indians had left Loving's Bend—as the place in the
river is now called—the morning after Wilson's
departure. Then Loving, instead of going down
the river as he had said he would do, went up. He
dragged himself about five miles before stopping
in a narrow pass between a mountain and the river.
There he remained for five days and was chewing
on a glove when some Mexicans found him. It
was 150 miles to Fort Sumner and Loving gave
the Mexicans $150 to take him there in their cart.

When Goodnight arrived, Loving was walking about, but the wound in his arm was not doing well. He had not received proper medical attention. Gangrene set in and nine days after Goodnight's arrival he died.

Knowing that the year's business would show a loss, on his death bed Loving asked his partner to maintain the partnership business until enough money was made to put his family on their feet. Goodnight promised. Loving was buried. Then Goodnight went on up into Colorado.

In January he returned, exhumed the coffin, and either he or Loving's son drove it 600 miles to Weatherford, Texas. A year or two later he turned over to the Loving estate half the profits he had made following the death of his "old pardner."

15

Inspectors and Holdups

Before a herd left the county of its origin it was
required by law to be inspected. For cattle not
in his brand the owner was required to have proper
bills-of-sale. He often produced bogus bills-of-sale.
The inspector often seemed more interested in
collecting his fee than in anything else.

The cattle also were required to be road-
branded. A herd of a thousand cattle might be
made up from dozens of purchases, each in a
different brand. If one road-brand was burned

into all of them, any animal that came into the herd on the way north could be easily distinguished as not belonging there. Some owners took along branding irons and road-branded what they could pick up. They were considered thieves by the great majority of trail men, but they existed.

After trail driving became well established, big cowmen kept inspectors, called "trail cutters," at the Red River crossings and elsewhere to look for their brands in passing herds and cut out any cattle wearing them. Organization came finally, but cowmen were by nature and experience against surrendering anything of self dependence to communal action. It is a wonder that in a continent of unfenced land and constant movement, more stolen cattle were not driven away than were.

"Stray in the herd and boss said kill it," runs a line of the "Song of the Chisholm Trail." Many a boss and owner with strays in his herd drove around inspection points, just as a "wanted" man with a herd separated himself from it, to rejoin it after it was past searching eyes.

Illegitimate claimers gave honest trail drivers about as much trouble as legal inspectors gave cattle thieves. They flourished in the Indian Territory, where Branch Isbell encountered a typical gang in 1876. This was the first herd Isbell had bossed, although he had driven up the trail several times. As a twelve-year-old boy in Alabama during the Civil War he had seen a squad of Confederate soldiers driving 300 long-legged, immense-horned steers from Texas and had then resolved to go to Texas when he was "big" and be a cowboy. But a six-shooter was never a part of his ambition, and in old age he often said that his life had been saved several times by not having one.

He did not have a six-shooter when, after a night stampede about forty miles north of Red River Station, he found thirty big steers missing from his herd. Leaving all hands with the cattle but an old Mexican vaquero, who was also unarmed, he and this vaquero headed south to find the missing animals. They found the hide of one that had been butchered. Then, going on down the trail, they found the others in a pen, along with twelve steers in another road brand and ten cows.

In front of a cabin a little way off Isbell saw a woman sweeping the yard with a bundle of broomweeds. Before interviewing her he scribbled on a piece of paper a legal-looking power of attorney to handle the twelve steers. He carried papers for his own brand in his pocket.

Then he told the woman that twenty-nine steers

Before they had driven the cattle half a mile, ten

in the pen belonged to him, that he had authority
to take twelve other steers there, and that he was
going to take the cows also, as they belonged to
some trail man. The woman said he had better
wait for her husband. She said that he and some
other men were gathering stampeded cattle for
trail men. She didn't add that they were professional stampeders.

Branch Isbell and his vaquero did not wait, but
before they had driven the cattle half a mile, ten
tough-looking, heavily-armed men emerged from
brush and surrounded them. "I looked innocent
and felt scared," Branch Isbell related, "but after
about thirty minutes of bluff on their part and
diplomatic talk on mine, we agreed that they could

armed men emerged from brush and surrounded them

keep the ten cows as payment for penning the steers." After driving the steers thirty miles they put them in the herd to which at least the majority belonged.

Kansas grangers were not usually thieves but they gave the trailmen lots of trouble. According to Kansas law, a furrow about a homesteader's land was the equivalent of a fence. Passing cattle did not so regard it. Often the granger demanded damages for trespassing, but he might be mollified if the trail boss agreed to bed his herd handily to the squatter's dugout—so that cowchips would be left there for fuel.

After crossing Smoky Hill River, Gus Black, bossing a herd for a big operator named Lytle, was confronted by a "jackleg lawyer" who demanded fifty dollars as toll for passing through the community of grangers he represented. He said that the charge was made for "inspecting against contagious diseases" in the cattle.

This was no place to have a herd held up. "I don't have any money," Gus Black told the jackleg lawyer and his accomplices, "but I'll give you a draft on Captain Lytle." Oh, yes, Lytle's check was good anywhere, but would Mr. Black add ten dollars for tobacco for the community? Black wrote the check for sixty dollars. A few days later he was within reach of a telegraph station and wired his employer that he had been buncoed out of sixty dollars and to refuse to pay the draft. Lytle paid it anyhow. It represented one of the comparatively inexpensive annoyances of the trail.

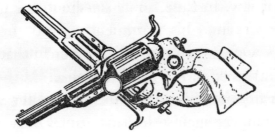

16

Six-Shooters and Cow Towns

According to Anglo-American tradition, all men are equal before the law. Private power might at times warp the law, and mob violence might occasionally overpower it, but for hundreds of years the tradition has made legal justice and the English language synonyms. But on the far rims of American frontiers often there was, temporarily, no organization of society or government and no law.

At the very time when Western frontiers were

advancing with most vigor, Colonel Samuel Colt's revolving pistol came into use. The saying arose that Colonel Colt made all men equal—taking the place of law. In time, some six-shooters had mottoes expressing this sentiment carved on ivory handles. One motto ran: "Fear no man that walks beneath the skies, for I will equalize."

The first notable use of the six-shooter was by Texas rangers against Indians armed only with a few muzzle-loading rifles and bows and arrows. The power of men on horseback to shoot five or six times without stopping to reload utterly demoralized the Indians. Other frontiersmen were not slow in arming themselves with Colt's invention.

Most early-day cowboys wore six-shooters. Some trail drivers carried rifles in scabbards as well as six-shooters, but a scabbarded gun is a hindrance to cow work and the great majority of trail men did not carry rifles. Cattle stealing on the open range called forth far more action with both six-shooter and rifle than trail work did. In 1883 an outfit of fifteen men driving a herd from San Marcos, Texas, to Dodge City had only three six-shooters.

Primarily, the six-shooter was worn not to kill, but to protect and enforce what the wearer regarded as justice. Bat Masterson, who became noted among cowboys as a peace officer at Dodge City, arrived at that frontier outpost ahead of Texas longhorns and contracted to grade a mile of railroad right-of-way for $300. While he was finishing the job, the man who owed him left the country. Masterson was only nineteen years old, and he was "broke." One day a friend told him that his debtor was coming through Dodge City on a train with a roll of greenbacks. Masterson met the train, boarded it, found the man, and persuaded him to come outside onto the platform. Then, showing him the muzzle of his six-shooter, he said, "If you don't pay me that $300 you'll never get back on that train." The man pulled out a roll of bills tied with a buckskin string and peeled off $300. Colonel Colt had "equalized."

A bully was not likely to try to run over a man with a six-shooter, but six-shooters brought out the bullying instinct in many men. As added power, it made many cowboys who were not at all "gunmen" reckless. It did not make a cowboy a bad man, though many people in the north who saw cowboys fresh off the trail from Texas wearing six-shooters and heard them shooting—mostly for fun—regarded them as ruffians, outlaws, Western bad men.

Contrary to the flaming covers of Wild West magazines and novels, few trail drivers saw the flash of six-shooters in front of stampedes. A quavering call known as the Texas lullaby was far more effective in soothing the frightened animals than popping, flashing six-shooters. No real cowman wanted six-shooter action around his cattle.

Many cowboys carried six-shooters because it was stylish to carry them, pretty much as army officers on parade carried swords long after the sword ceased to be used as a weapon in battle. The six-shooter was a kind of badge indicating that its bearer followed a proud occupation. Plenty of cowboys were good shots, and a few had bored daylight into man targets, but many were poor marksmen and seldom shot their six-shooters. My uncle Frank Byler, for whom I am named, went up the trail with a herd of horses in the 1880s wearing a six-shooter that he did not pull out of its holster until one day in the Indian Territory while his horse was drinking at a stagnant pool. From the saddle he saw a moccasin in the water and drew to shoot it. The trigger or hammer had become so clotted with dirt and rust that he could not cock the gun. Thereupon he threw it in disgust at the snake and left it in the mud. He realized, he said, that unless a man could use a six-shooter he had better be without one.

One of the shooting places for cowboys was Doan's Store, just south of Red River on the Dodge City Trail. Here C. F. Doan and his brother sold everything from tucking combs to whiskey, kept a restaurant, welcomed preachers, subscribed to the *London Graphic,* read Dickens to their children, and in the trailing season employed a cowboy to call the nightly square dances. The Doans aimed to attract trade from trail outfits camping in the region and sometimes waiting for days for a big rise in Red River to go down before crossing. Millions of longhorns passed that way.

C. F. Doan told me that one night a cowboy named Joe Dameron shot 175 times; another cowboy kept count. Dameron would empty his cartridge belt, go into the store and buy another belt full. He had a good deal of whiskey under his belt and was "just celebrating." He shot into the ground or into the air. Many cowboys and trail cutters hanging around the store in daytime would practice shooting at cottonwood trees, but often, Doan said, "They shot just to hear their pistols pop rather than to perfect marksmanship." After the great trail was plowed under and fenced across, Doan sold the saloon building for the lumber in it, to be moved away. The flooring was so full of bullet holes that it was worthless. One year Doan picked up enough bullet lead around the store to weight a new sixty-foot seine.

It took a lot of talking to prevent trouble among some of the drinkers, but the only man ever killed at Doan's was the manager of a ranch on Red River. Texas rangers tried to arrest him. He jumped on his horse and as he was galloping away was shot in the back. Three months after he was killed and buried, incensed cowboys got a preacher to hold services at his grave and then passed a hat to reward the preacher. It was filled with silver dollars.

Doan used to tell with pride that he had never lost a dollar through credit to trail men, whether he filled up a chuck wagon with groceries or fitted a cowboy with Indian-made buckskin gloves. Sometimes it might be a year or more before a debtor sent or brought the money, but the trail men who bought from him were not deadbeats. He left the store unlocked at night, and many a passing cowboy went in, took off his six-shooter belt, and slept on a blanket unrolled on the counter.

When young men—very young most of them

were got to a cow town after months on the trail, received their pay, and in companywith each other started out to "see the elephant," they often felt obliged to show off and startle the natives. One citizen in Dodge City said he tired of hearing the "everlasting clinking of cowboy spurs." Wyatt Earp, city marshal, boasted that in making arrests for disturbing the peace he had "made a dent in cowboy conceit." Not all cowboys drank whiskey when they got to town, but the noisiest among them had usually tanked up on "brave-maker." There was nothing they enjoyed more than emptying their six-shooters into the air as they galloped out of town.

A. J. Sowell, who ranged with range men in dangerous times and wrote realistically of them, said in his *Rangers and Pioneers of Texas* (1884): "Occasionally in some western village you will hear a voice ring out on the night air in words like these: 'Wild and woolly,' 'Hard to hold,' 'Raised a pet but gone wild,' 'Walked the Chisholm Trail backwards,' 'Fought Indians and killed buffalo,' 'Hide out, little ones.'" A listener of the times might also have heard in the night air, "Born high up on the Guadalupe, raised on thorny prickly pear, quarreled with alligators and tussled with grizzly bears," or "Raised in a canebrake, suckled

by a she bear, and the click of a six-shooter is music
to me ear. The higher up the creek you go, the
worse they get, and I come from the head of it."

After all the yelling, a few shots might be expected. It was a cowboy or two on a spree. Nobody likely was hurt. A friend who was sober relieved any shooter of his pistol and soon all was
quiet.

Such action did not express viciousness, thirst
for blood, or gangster greed. It was a letting off
of steam. When the steam was let off in Kansas,
however, and some Kansas peace officer tried to
stop it, the result might be hot-blooded resistance.
The trail drivers of Confederate tradition clanned
together when they got off their range in a northern cow town. The only resorts were saloons and
dance halls. There many cowboys simply lost
their heads.

There was so little outlawry among the original trail drivers that Abilene, Kansas, did not in-
corporate and employ a peace officer until after
three seasons of cattle driving to it had passed. In
1870 it had thirty-two licensed saloons, the most
prominent being the Alamo; it had also the Devil's
Addition, beyond the city limits. Then the city
council began the construction of a jail on Texas
Street. One night cowboys roped the timbers and

After months on the trail, cowboys liked to celebrate

dragged them away. They were reassembled and the jail was built. The first person put into it was a Negro trail cook from an outfit holding cattle near town. All the cook had done was get a little gay from the tarantula juice served in one of the saloons. The cowboys he had fed all the way up from Texas came into town, drove the guards away from the jail, knocked the lock open and took their cook back to camp.

Then Abilene got a town marshal named Tom Smith. He posted a sign in the Alamo and other places saying that firearms were to be "deposited with the proprietor," to be retrieved when the owner was ready to leave town. Tom Smith seems not to have had much trouble enforcing the rule. He was killed by a Kansas homesteader—not by a cowboy.

In 1871, Wild Bill Hickok came as marshal. He was a long-haired, gun-flashing showman. He murdered Phil Coe, who was celebrating with some other Texans. The next year Abilene ceased to be a cow town. The cowboys had made it lively as well as prosperous, but they had not shown in the whole time of bringing cattle to Abilene the kind of toughness associated with murderous, holdup racketeers of modern times.

As the trailing of cattle advanced and vast new ranges were stocked, many men not native to the range joined cowboy outfits. Some of them were outlaws, but Billy the Kid, Sam Bass and other notorious gunmen who operated on horseback were never representative cowboys. Here is an incident representative of bad-man behavior in a trail outfit.

With a herd coming up to Dodge City in 1877 was a hand who called himself William Samples. As became known later, he had killed a man in Arkansas, skipped to Texas, and assumed the Samples name. He was suspicious of all strangers, fancying that any man who came to the herd was looking for him. He came near killing a new hand hired by the boss on the trail.

One day while the herd was being held near Dodge City, the boss hired an eighteen-year-old Kansas cowboy named Enos Moseley to replace one of his men who had quit. About two o'clock the next morning Samples shot him dead in his sleep. Samples jumped on his horse and ran off. He was soon wounded and captured by three bona fide cowboys and before he died confessed that he killed Moseley because he took him to be a nephew of the man murdered in Arkansas. Samples was a deficient-minded criminal; he drove cattle up the trail and wore a six-shooter like other trail men, but neither in using it nor in character did he represent the trail drivers.

Abilene, Ellsworth, Caldwell, Hays, Newton, Junction, all in Kansas, had their day as cow towns on the trail from Texas. Ogallala in Nebraska, Cheyenne in Wyoming, and Miles City in Montana were made boisterous by many a cowboy just off the trail. But the cow town of all cow towns was Dodge City on the Arkansas. It received the most cows and the most cowboys over the longest period of time that any shipping and delivery point for Texas cattle received. Also it was the toughest.

It was started by bootleggers who camped there to sell liquor to soldiers of Fort Dodge four and a half miles down the river. The coming of the Santa Fe Railroad in 1872 made it a town. The coming of Texas cattle made it for ten years the biggest cattle market in the world.

Its supreme toughness came largely from buffalo hunters, bullwhackers, muleskinners and horse thieves and from professional gamblers, confidence men, and other preyers upon country men who earned their money. The town officials were saloon keepers and gamblers. Plenty of range men were tough, but if they were the kind who "hung with them longhorn cattle" they were separated by a deep gulf from the slick money-grabbers.

17

Trail's End

In 1873 the Missouri, Kansas and Pacific Railroad, building south, reached Denison, Texas, just below Red River. Within a few years it connected San Antonio and other points downstate with Chicago. But neither this railroad nor any of its successors interfered with trail driving so long as there was open country to trail through. It was far cheaper to drive the longhorned walkers than to ship them. After Texas land crossed by the old trails had been fenced, tens of thousands of cattle and horses were shipped to Denison, Wichita Falls,

Vernon, and other towns adjacent to Red River, and then driven on north.

The first fences were of planks, pickets, rocks, slick wire, hedge growth. They were mostly to fence cattle *out* of cultivated fields and to enclose small pastures for saddle horses. Fencing cattle *into* big pastures followed the introduction of barbed wire in 1875, but it was several years later before many ranches were enclosed. The first extensive fencing was on the original breeding grounds of the longhorns, in southern Texas. The last rangelands to be enclosed were owned by the government and by Indian tribes in the Rocky Mountain states.

As a result of this progress in the stretching of barbed wire, the last trail herds out of Texas did not originate in the longhorn country but on the western edge of the state, where Herefords had already displaced longhorns. The trail they followed, last of all the long cattle trails, skirted the Rocky Mountains west of Kansas, leading through Colorado and Wyoming into Montana. It was called the Northern Trail, also the Montana Trail. By 1895 it was very difficult to get a herd over it.

By 1886 farmers were in control of western Kansas and the always-threatening quarantine against ticky Texas cattle was extended to shut them off from Dodge City. Law or no law, the time had come when the only economical course for any rancher to follow was to fence in his pastures, drill wells, erect windmills, and breed up his cattle.

Despite vitality, self-reliance, rustling abilities and other qualities that adapted the longhorns to frontier conditions, they sometimes died in great numbers from starvation. That was after the ranges became too over-stocked to afford grass during long drouths. That was also while land and cattle were cheap.

The day of the trail driver was coming to an end

Until an owner could control his own land, keep his own cattle on it and keep other people's cattle off it, he could not afford to improve it. As land and beef advanced in prices, it was no longer economic to pasture or to feed hay, grain, cottonseed products, or anything else to longhorn cattle. They ate as much as better bred cattle but produced less meat.

Gradually the cows were crossed on pure-bred bulls, the horns, bodies and legs all growing shorter, the whole frame becoming heavier with meat. The United States government preserves a herd of longhorns, alongside a herd of buffaloes, on the Wichita Wildlife Refuge in Oklahoma. It is a "museum piece." A few rangemen out of sentiment also keep some relics of the cattle that made the long trails and were at one time synonymous with Texas.

As long as Western lands grow grass but do not receive enough rainfall to make farming practicable, there will be cattle ranches and cowboys. Their day has not ended, but with the passing of the longhorns and the long trails they beat out, the most dramatic life that the grass lands of the world have known ended.

Index

179